The Sale Is in the Tale

*5 Storytelling Secrets to Keep
from Drowning in a Sea of Sameness*

John Livesay

Tradecraft Books, Los Angeles 90046

Printed in the United States of America
ISBN: 979-8-9854497-0-9
Livesay, John
The Sale Is in the Tale: 5 Storytelling Secrets to Keep from Drowning in a Sea
of Sameness
Book cover: Sergio Belletini
Author photo: Marcella Kerwin

Praise for *The Sale Is in the Tale*

In sales, how much of what you say is remembered? The answer is not much. Which means you haven't closed the deal. *The Sale Is in the Tale* is a game-changer. This fun-to-read story is a roadmap to how to become a black belt in storytelling so you (and your team) will be both memorable and magnetic.

> **Nina Lawrence**, Chief Content & Revenue Officer, Tinybeans
> Former VP Global Marketing & Content, Wall Street Journal

If you are in business, you are in sales. And of course in sales, you are in the storytelling business! This book is about empathy and listening as the access to telling your story with power and effectiveness.

> **Claudio Ludovisi**, Assistant Dean, Marketing, Strategy, and Corporate Relations, Pepperdine Graziadio Business School

One of the biggest challenges companies have is growing clients across divisions. *The Sale Is in the Tale* not only helps you win new business but also shows you how to break down silos using the power of storytelling. This book is your revenue roadmap.

> **Alyce Alston**, President, Eye Just
> Former CEO, De Beers

I share my story of how I created Pictionary all over the world, and John has helped me craft my stories and make them accessible, relevant, and relatable. My impact on the world has gone up tenfold by using John's coaching and using the tools from this book.

> **Rob Angel**, Creator, Pictionary
> Best-selling author, *Game Changer*

We all love a great story. How about a story about storytelling? Even better! Storytelling is a successful salesperson's superpower. This book demystifies the complex and layered benefits of adding stories to your customer journey… a great read for salespeople, sales teams, and sales managers.

Beth Cuzzone, Chief Strategic Growth Officer, Goulston & Storrs

John has always been a master storyteller, but his new book is something special. It's not just any run-of-the-mill read; the situations he writes about are relatable and inspiring because they're so detailed - you can't help but feel like there was an 'I' in this memoir as well! And who doesn't enjoy getting insight into other people?

Tony Grebmeier, CEO, ShipOffers

Much like building a home, telling a great story requires a blueprint and a solid foundation. *The Sale Is in the Tale* explains how to systematically build your story so you can better draw in your potential buyers with your solution--and win more sales!

Isaac Lidsky, CEO, Rigor

Behind every great gift is a story. Both gifts and stories build emotional connections and relationships which is the key when you are selling anything including yourself. *The Sale Is in the Tale* is not only a fascinating fable that is entertaining and intriguing but also shows you how to become a black belt in storytelling.

John Ruhlin, Best-selling author, Giftology
Founder & CEO, Ruhlin Group

John Livesay does it again! For years, corporate clients have hired him to be a keynote speaker to their sales teams to teach them the power of storytelling. Now he's crafted a fable, *The Sale Is in the Tale*. This book is everything you want a good story to be…intriguing, entertaining, and informative, while showing us all how to not drown in the sea of sameness anymore. Treat yourself to this fable and learn how to be persuasive without being pushy.

Josh Linkner, Venture capitalist, Five-time tech entrepreneur,
New York Times Best-selling author

John Livesay has been teaching top sales teams how to use the power of story to influence human behavior for decades. His latest book, *The Sale Is in the Tale*, is a powerful and entertaining fable that teaches readers how to become master storytellers. A must-read for everyone!

Daniel Burrus, *New York Times* bestselling author of seven books including *Flash Foresight* and *The Anticipatory Organization*

Throughout my years working with John Livesay, his reputation as The Pitch Whisperer proved itself time and time again. Livesay is the person you want on your team when the task before you is persuasion. Now, with *The Sale Is in the Tale*, his sense of wit, empathy, and storytelling acumen is on full display yet again. Enjoy a few moments with this book and the indispensable lessons it contains. You will be grateful you did.

Kenneth P. Baker FIIDA, Assoc. American Institute of Architects, Assoc. American Society of Interior Designers, SBID

Stories that are immersive and take you on a journey are the ones that tug at our heartstrings. *The Sale Is in the Tale* is a fable you'll remember and use often to increase your emotional connection with clients.

Amber Allen, Founder CEO Double A Labs

If you are looking for practical and reliable advice to improve your ability to sell— look no further than this enjoyable read. The Pitch Whisperer, John Livesay, provides actionable tips to apply the art of storytelling to establish a lasting connection with your customers. Inside you will find a helpful roadmap for building confidence and creating a victorious mindset that will underpin your next successful sales pitch.

Sameer Somal, CEO & Co-Founder, Blue Ocean Global Technology

Table of Contents

Foreword

In the world of sales, nobody gets a second-place medal. Whether we think it or not, we are all in sales. When we are trying to convince our spouse to fix a leaky faucet or attempting to ask our boss if we can work from home on Fridays, we are in sales. Or perhaps you're a scientist trying to get additional funding for your research. Or someone trying to get a friend to attend church. The PTA volunteer trying to raise money for the school field trip is also selling. Or maybe you're trying to convince your dad to stop smoking. The old adage that "we are all in sales" is an old adage because it's true.

However, some of us make our living from sales. We have quotas to meet and people to please. Many of us, in varying industries, must pitch ourselves and our products and services daily. We often face staunch competition with our greatest competitor in this day and age: getting and keeping someone's attention. Attention is the new oil.

One common complaint some salespeople have is "I'm so tired of coming in second place." They don't understand why they are not the *first* choice. The problem is that most of us are drowning in a sea of sameness, pitching speeds and feeds or stats that nobody remembers or really cares about.

Influence, a sale, getting people to act. These don't start in the head; they start in the heart. When Steve Jobs launched the iPod, he didn't talk about numerical processing speeds and storage capacity. His tale was simply "1,000 songs in your pocket."

The Sale Is in the Tale is a fable that takes you on a journey, where you will learn how to pull people in with stories that tug at their heartstrings, which cause people to open their purse strings. As with any good story, you will be entertained and immersed in wondering *What will happen next?* And after reading it, you will be inspired to start telling your own stories in a whole new way.

The number one problem I have seen while researching my book *The Focus Project* is that people don't know *how* to focus and *stay* focused. This certainly applies to salespeople who ramble, bore, and confuse potential buyers. John Livesay's book shows readers how to tell clear, concise, and compelling stories. Stories that sell.

You will become like a jukebox or playlist, having the ability to pull out the right story to tell at the right time to the right person. This transforms you into becoming magnetic and memorable.

Storytelling not only helps you in your career, but also helps you make better emotional connections in your personal life, too! Plato said, "Those who tell stories rule society." It is just as true today as it was then. Maybe even more so, since Plato didn't have to compete with the internet and social media to keep people's attention. Read this book and you will start telling stories that sell, today.

Erik Qualman
Five-time #1 International Best-selling Author & Speaker
Equalman.com

Introduction

Storytelling has been around at least since humans lived in caves. Our ancestors would sit around the glow of fires and tell stories. More recently, we sit around the glow of PowerPoint slides. Hopefully, we are hearing good stories, too, rather than just seeing crowded slides with facts and figures that nobody can read or will remember.

The **myth** is that people make decisions about what to buy or who to hire based on logical facts. This myth causes many people to think that soft skills, such as storytelling, listening, and being empathetic, are not worth investing their time or energy. The old way of selling, or persuading, was to push out facts and data to convince people you have the best product or service. We have seen that this does not cause anyone to change their mind in business, in politics, or in their personal life.

The *winning* **formula** is:
Storytelling + *listening* + *empathy* = an *emotional connection*

People buy *emotionally* and then back it up with logic.

We can see that, for example, in people who want to make a change in their personal lives. Maybe they want to cut sugar from their diet. There is no shortage of information about why we should limit sugar intake, and we certainly don't need *more* information to help us eat better. Yet the decision about whether to eat a dessert is not often backed by logic, but by *happy* emotions. Think about eating an ice cream cone on a hot summer day. There are usually *emotional* reasons that cause people to want to escape anxiety or overindulge to stuff down feelings.

We see this time and time again in political campaigns. The candidate that pushes out details of their many policies to fix things will most likely lose to the one that has an overall story that tugs at people's emotions, such as patriotism.

Yet in sales in the business world, so many executives ignore these human examples of the power of storytelling and revert to the old way of self-promotion. The first mistake is that they forget they are not invited into a pitch to tell potential buyers how great they are, but they are instead invited in to help them solve some type of problem that has a sense of urgency to it. The problem could be anything from a way to break through the noise of a crowded marketplace with a new launch, or how to find a product that makes a hospital more productive and deliver better patient outcomes during surgery.

Whether you are a hospital executive, surgeon, lawyer, architect, financial services provider, or creator of the latest product using state-of-the-art technology, you need to figure out a way to stand out and command a premium price. Those who present facts are seen as a commodity and cause people to go into "analysis paralysis," which is when an individual can't make a decision because they continue to analyze all the facts. Those who tell stories tap into the part of the buyers' brains that can sum up the concept and make a decision.

One of the real benefits of becoming a black belt in storytelling is the ability to have other people remember your story for the "meeting after the meeting." Most pitches that are dominated by facts about things like how long the company has been around, how many offices you have, or the "speeds and feeds" features of a tech product are quickly forgotten. When clients then have their own private meeting after they have heard all the pitches, they say, "They all sound the same, let's go with the cheapest price."

Those salespeople who come into a pitch/interview/bake-off where they are in the final three against their competitors and *tell stories* are the ones who typically win the sale. When potential buyers can remember and repeat your story to others, they become your inside brand ambassadors. The best way to make sure they do that is to tell a story that they see themselves in. This pulls them in, and then they want to go on the same journey with you.

Many people tell me they believe some people are natural-born storytellers and some are not. The people who say this are usually in the camp of not feeling like they are natural-born storytellers. The good news is that, unlike becoming a professional athlete or singer, you do not have to have a huge God-given talent to learn how to tell a great story. There is a *proven process* you will learn in this book that will make you a better storyteller in both your personal and professional life. For those of you who think you are a great storyteller, you will see how to get yourself up to the gold medal level.

This book is a fable that is really a story about the **power of storytelling**. Many of the situations are taken from my years of selling and working with sales' teams on all the frustrations of losing a sale and not knowing what went wrong. Like any good story, there are twists and turns that will have you rooting for the hero, learning from the mentor, and watching how nonlinear the journey of success can truly be.

This book is designed to be an entertaining way to immerse yourself in the story and learn along with the characters how to make your career and life better by mastering storytelling skills.

This book is for:

- Anyone who has to sell themselves to get a job or promotion or get their ideas implemented
- Anyone who has dealt with rejection in their career and took it personally
- Anyone who went for a promotion and didn't get it and wondered why
- Anyone who is tired of coming in second place when they must pitch against competitors
- Anyone who is struggling to communicate their value proposition in a way that is not all numbers and facts
- Anyone looking for a new way to create a sense of urgency when someone's making a decision about whether or not to buy from them
- Anyone looking for a way to get off the self-esteem roller coaster of only feeling good if your numbers are up and feeling bad if they're down
- Anyone looking for a step-by-step way to become a black belt in storytelling
- Anyone who is tired of playing defense when they have to defend themselves against their competition to potential buyers
- Anyone looking for new ways to develop rapport and start conversations with strangers
- Anyone looking for a way to get the potential buyers from just saying "I'm interested" to saying "I'm in"
- Anyone who's looking for a way to go from being seen as an annoying pest to a welcome guest
- Anyone looking for new ways to keep potential buyers engaged when presenting
- Anyone looking for a new way to be persuasive without being pushy

Divisions within a company are often in silos. They don't share connections or stories or information. Storytelling can become part of your culture, which can help you not only win new business but onboard new team members and break down silos so you can grow existing clients.

It is time to start making your soft skills stronger.

At the end of the day, whoever tells the best story wins the sale. The Sale Is in the Tale!

Nobody is successful alone, and there are many people who have been my mentors along the way. Acknowledgments are in the back of the book, but none of us can really thank the people enough who help us along our journey.

The Sale Is in the Tale

Exposition

Sweat drips from Ben's forehead as he stabs at the keyboard. The conference room seems to close in on him, and he can feel his boss, Carl, staring into the back of his head. There are no windows in the stuffy room, and everyone sits in complete silence waiting for him to fix the video. The tension gets worse and worse as the seconds pass, and Ben gets more and more anxious. He is uncomfortable with the silence and finds himself filling it with sounds like "Ummm," "Hmmm," and "Urgggg."

No one responds.

Earlier that day, Carl and Ben sat on an equally stuffy flight from Austin to Houston to pitch their company's newest medical equipment product, the Lightning Scalpel, to MD Anderson Cancer Center. MD Anderson is one of the leading hospitals in the country, and they have been trying to get an appointment with them for a while now. They finally received the call last week that they could fit Ben in as one of three companies to pitch their equipment in just a few days.

Though Ben was the salesperson assigned to the Lightning Scalpel, his boss Carl felt it was necessary that he come, too, to show how important the client is to them. Ben didn't know what to think when he got that email from Kara, Carl's assistant:

Hi, Ben!

Carl is going to be attending the MD Anderson pitch meeting with you next week. As you know, this client really means a lot to us, and Carl thinks it'll make a good impression if he's there, too.

He said to remind you, again, how big this is for Athena and said specifically for me to tell you, "Don't mess this up."

Talk soon!
Kara

Ben struggled to make small talk with Carl on the flight. When he asked what Carl's been watching on TV lately, Carl briefly spoke about the LA Dodgers, and Ben tried to nod and make affirmative noises until he finally had to admit that he knew nothing about sports. It was right about then that Carl put on his headphones and didn't look towards Ben until they landed.

As if Ben needed any more confirmation that Carl isn't his biggest fan.

Carl walked around the hallways of Athena as if he owned the place, in his expensive suit and criticisms about every little thing. One time, Ben was at his desk on a sales call, and Carl was walking by. He actually came over and made Ben put the call on hold while he attacked Ben's sales techniques and told him "how to do it properly." Ben was humiliated.

And now, Carl is sitting across from Ben, as Ben struggles to get the video to play at the MD Anderson meeting.

Ben worked tirelessly on the video ever since he learned about the Lightning Scalpel. He met with Diane, the senior solutions engineer, every other day. They would go over the specs and the processes, and Diane explained every single aspect of the Scalpel. Ben was confident that he knew it inside and outside. Diane taught him everything he had to know to get this thing sold.

And now, here they are, stuffed into what feels like an MD Anderson supply closet, with two junior executives waiting to watch *the* video that is supposed to win him this sale.

The "junior executive" part was enough to send Carl into a tailspin before they even got into the room. Ben called MD Anderson last Friday to confirm that their VP of Operations would be there in the meeting, and he was assured that she would be.

But things happen, and she had "an emergency" this morning, so her two juniors were filling in for her. Carl was indignant that he flew all the way to this meeting and wouldn't even be sitting with the real decision makers, and of course, that was somehow Ben's fault.

But they have a bigger problem on their hands now, as the Wi-Fi is apparently too weak in the supply-closet-turned-conference-room for the video to play.

One of the junior executives in the corner clears her throat. "You must have it saved locally, too, right? Maybe you can pull it up from your downloads."

Carl shuffles in his seat and makes a noise that almost sounds like a muffled laugh.

Ben looks towards Carl quickly and then back to the woman. "Uh, well no. Not exactly. I uploaded the video to Vimeo from my desktop, so it's not available on my laptop here," he replies.

"Oh," the executive replies, almost apologetically.

Finally defeated, Ben straightens and wipes his brow. He takes a quick sip from his glass of water and tries to pivot. "I know the Lightning

Scalpel like the back of my hand, anyway. Why don't I just talk to you about it?"

He launches into a pretty good description of the Scalpel, including the impressive statistics given to him from R&D. He eventually finds his stride after being thrown off by the video incident, and the junior executives seem impressed when he tells them that Lightning Scalpel can reduce time in surgery by 30%, much to the benefit of both the doctor and the patient.

By the time they shake hands and walk out of the closet, Ben is almost feeling good about himself. That is, until he turns and sees Carl's red face looming over him.

"What. Was. That?!" Carl roared.

"I know, I should have had the video," Ben says, shaking his head.

"Yes! You should have had the video!"

There are two men walking ahead of Ben and Carl, and they visibly jump when Carl yells. When they turn to see where the voice is coming from, Ben quickly looks down to avoid eye contact.

He quietly responds, "But they seemed happy with the information I gave them. I have a really good feeling about it."

Carl doesn't meet Ben's soft tone. "Oh, do you? A good feeling? Maybe you didn't see the yawns that I saw when you were on the number tirade."

Ben looks up, shocked by what Carl said. "What? No way! Those numbers are super impressive. That's what's going to close the sale!"

"Yes. Now those *juniors* need to remember those numbers to report back to their boss, who was conveniently unavailable today since you didn't confirm!" Carl continues yelling.

"I told you, I did conf---." Ben stops there, dejected. There is no use in arguing anymore at this point.

Plus, they still have the entire flight home to sit in uncomfortable, and disapproving, silence.

Problem

"Yikes," Diane says sympathetically as Ben recounts the MD Anderson meeting to her the next afternoon.

Ben is sitting hunched in his desk chair. Diane stands across from him, leaning on the cubical wall, shaking her head.

"I know. I worked really hard on that pitch," Ben responds. "I don't get it. Those numbers are *so* impressive, but Carl still seems to think they won't bite."

"Maybe if we went over your pitch together? I could try to weigh in and offer some advice," Diane suggests.

Just then, Ben's desk phone rings, and when he picks it up, it's Carl's assistant, Kara.

"Hey, Ben. Carl wants to see you."

"Now?" he asks.

"I definitely wouldn't make him wait," she responds.

"On my way," Ben says before hanging up.

He looks at Diane as he hangs up the phone. "Thanks for the offer to listen to the pitch. I'll definitely take you up on that, but I have to run now. That was Kara. I guess Carl wants to see me."

Ben shuffles out of his cubicle, past Diane. "If I'm not back in an hour, call the police," Ben jokes over his shoulder.

"It was nice knowing you," she replies, trying to lighten the mood.

Walking down the hallway to Carl's office feels like walking to the principal's office. Ben gets that familiar pit in his stomach, as if he did something wrong.

He greets Kara when he turns the corner, and she jumps up to usher Ben into Carl's office and quickly shuts the door behind him.

Carl's office is big and sterile. He sits in a large leather chair behind an even larger desk with just a small MacBook before him.

He is typing something and doesn't look up when Ben enters. Ben takes it upon himself to sit in the closest of the three chairs across from the desk.

"Hey, Carl. How's it going?" He tries to sound casual.

Carl finally looks away from his screen, peering at Ben over the top of the laptop. "We did *not* get the MD Anderson deal." He says gruffly. "But that shouldn't be a surprise."

Ben feels the room start to spin.

"We didn't?" he asks meekly, finding it hard to form a complete thought.

"Nope. And their exec didn't even call me to tell me herself. One of those juniors called. Incredibly embarrassing," Carl responds.

Ben leans forward and puts his head in his hands. "Carl, I'm so sorry. I really thought--"

"Stop right there." Carl says, putting his hand out in front of him. "That's the problem. What you *think* will land us a sale just isn't working for you -- or us -- anymore."

Oof. Ben feels like he was punched in the gut.

Carl continues. "And I know you were looking forward to that promotion, but after losing this sale, there's no way I can give it to you. I wanted to tell you face-to-face. I gave the promotion to Julie. She's been on a good run lately, and she really has a way of being memorable during her pitches. She just has this… *authenticity* about her. People know that she's being herself, and she gets a lot of sales like that. They feel like they can trust her."

Ben tries to think of something to say but comes up blank. Authentic? How is he *not* being authentic? He was doing what everyone does, he thought: Sell the product! The numbers are real. Isn't that authentic?

As if reading his mind, Carl says, "I'm not saying that you are lying or being dishonest. But what you did is the same thing every other salesperson has ever done. It's hard for you to stand out to our clients when you're drowning in that sea of sameness."

Sea of sameness?

He really was relying on that promotion. He was hoping to buy a condo downtown and be closer to all the action of Austin. Maybe meet someone and be able to settle down. But without the promotion, and the raise that comes with it, he has to stay put in the small basement apartment he's been renting just outside of Austin for the foreseeable future.

And *Julie*?

She was hired a year after him. He helped train her up, and he never thought she would pass him for the promotion.

Ben then realizes that Carl had been staring at him, waiting for a response.

"Well… Okay. Like I said, I was really confident in that meeting, and even though the video didn't work, I thought the numbers could speak for themselves." Ben shakes his head in disbelief.

"The numbers are great!" Carl yelled. "But numbers are forgotten. Especially if they're not written on a screen. Or in a video."

Ouch.

"Ben, you were great a few years ago, but the industry is changing. Your last few sales appointments haven't been great, which is why I wanted to go with you to Houston. Because this one was so important. And now here we are. I'm not going to threaten you or anything. But… well… get those sales numbers up."

"Yes. Yes, I know. Okay. Thanks."

Why did I say thanks?, Ben thinks to himself. *Thanks for not firing me?*

Carl and Ben sit in an uncomfortable silence for 10 seconds until Ben realizes that was his cue to leave.

Carl watches him as he gets up. Ben tries to figure out what to say, but there's really nothing left to be said. Instead, he just slowly walks to the door and sees himself out.

Everything after the meeting with Carl feels like a blur. When Ben gets back to his cubicle, he stares at his blank computer screen and just hopes no one comes up behind him. He watches the clock count up to 5:00 p.m. and is out the door by 5:02.

Later that night, Ben sits in front of the TV eating the pizza that he picked up on the way home. He is trying to watch *Ted Lasso*, the show that everyone has been raving about, but he can't focus. All he can think about is work and losing that promotion.

What am I supposed to do?, he thinks. *This is all I've done since I graduated college. And I used to be good at it!*

Ben *did* used to be good at it. He wasn't top of his class at the University of Illinois or anything, but he never got below a B-. He worked hard in school, and his professors liked him.

He landed a great, sought-after internship at Athena Medical, the same company he works for now. The people he worked for as an intern saw his potential and offered him a junior position after graduation, and he slowly but steadily worked his way up the ranks to a senior account executive.

The goal was sales manager, though, and that was the job that he knew he would get if only he got the MD Anderson deal. That was the job that would put him in a different bracket. He would finally have people working for *him* rather than always being the low guy on the totem pole. He would get out of this basement apartment. He would meet someone, get married, and keep working his way up the ladder.

Ben often fell into the trap of comparing himself to others, ever since high school. While he didn't like sports, he certainly liked the attention and fame the quarterback received in his midwestern high school. He wanted to be great, but he always fell short when he compared himself to others.

Then when his 30th birthday came and went, he realized someone he went to college with had made the list of *Forbes* "30 under 30." It really hurt, how "behind" he felt compared to his peers.

When Ben was in school, remembering facts and numbers was one area where he really did excel, and it's probably what landed him his first job at Athena. When selling, he barely even needed any notes, as he proved in the MD Anderson meeting. He remembered the exact speed or storage capacity or percentage increase for everything he ever sold. And he knew how to make those numbers sound impressive, even when sometimes they weren't.

People loved working with him because of this. They could take a backseat during these sales calls and meetings and let Ben do what Ben does best: Recall those numbers and make them seem remarkable.

And now what? He can't go back to school. How is he supposed to learn a "new" way of selling products? And why isn't the old way of just pushing out facts and information good enough anymore?

While he stares at the TV without really listening to the dialogue, Ben remembers the Einstein definition of insanity: insanity is doing the same thing over and over again and expecting a different outcome.

Well, it's time to break the cycle.

Solution

Part 1

On Monday, Diane is waiting for Ben by his cubicle, armed with Starbucks. It's their Monday ritual. Ben realized a while ago that simple rituals like this bond people. Otherwise, we might as well be working with AI bots.

"Hey," she says, handing over the hot coffee (light with milk, one sugar). The cup says BEND rather than "Ben" on it.

"Hey," Ben grumbles in response as he sinks into his seat. He looks at the cup and sees they misspelled his name. "Bend," he says. "Is this some kind of message from the universe? Be flexible?"

Diane laughs. "Who knows? But don't look a gift horse in the mouth."

Diane waits for Ben to get settled and turn on his computer before saying, "I met Carl's assistant in the elevator last Friday. She told me what happened."

"Seriously? She is *such* a gossip!"

"Doesn't mean it didn't happen," Diane responds.

"Yep. Julie got the promotion."

Diane sighs and takes a sip from her own coffee (black).

Ben says, "I just don't understand. You explained everything about that Scalpel to me, and *I* was impressed! Why can't they see it? I spent the whole weekend panicking about the future. What am I supposed to do? Go back to school? Take a training course? I can't afford either option currently, and I was relying on that promotion to finally get out of the basement and move on with my life."

"Ben, calm down! Panicking doesn't ever help. I've had plenty of setbacks in the job, and even in my personal life. Remember my awful break-up last year? Have you ever, ever seen me panic?"

Ben thinks for a moment. "Actually… no. I never really thought about it, but you are one of the calmest people I know."

"Well, I wasn't always like this. I was a nervous wreck in college. I tried so hard to make everyone happy and prove myself. I was barely sleeping. My parents were constantly on my case. It's not easy being a first-generation American, and the first person in your family to go to college. I had so much to prove to everyone."

"So what changed?" Ben asks.

"My roommates were always having so much fun and seemed so relaxed about school. I told myself that it was because they didn't have the overbearing parents that I did, constantly asking about grades and homework and exams.

"But then one night when they were going out to a party and I stayed behind to study, one of them said, 'Diane, you know this test won't matter five years from now, right? It probably won't even matter five months from now.' For some reason, that really stuck with me. I actually came up with my own rule: the 5-5-5 rule. Now, whenever I get worried or upset or anxious about something, I ask myself, 'Will this matter in 5 minutes?' and a lot of the time, the answer is, 'Yes, this will still matter in 5 minutes.' So then I keep zooming out. What about 5 hours? 5 days? If the answer is still yes, I keep going. 5 months? 5 years? And eventually, the answer becomes 'No.'"

Ben is quiet, thinking about what Diane just said. "Hmm," he says. "I never thought of that."

Diane goes on. "Another way of thinking about it is this: We are the movie directors of our own lives, right? We have the power to call

'Cut!' at any time and re-focus. And because of that, we have three cameras at our disposal: The first is how *we* see things. What lens are you using? Is it a wide-angle or close-up lens? The second is the choice to see things from *others'* perspectives and the ability to show empathy for what they see and feel. And the third is the ability to *zoom out* and see the big picture. And this goes back to the 5-5-5 rule. Will this be important or stressful 5 minutes from now? How about 5 days or 5 years from now?"

She pauses, and Ben lets this sink in. Diane then continues. "And that's how I taught myself to not panic but to stay calm. Because it's true. That test didn't matter five weeks after, once the semester was over. And five years after college, I did find myself regretting stressing too much about my grades and not making enough friends."

Ben nods slowly and takes a sip of his coffee. Finally, he says, "I get it. But losing the MD Anderson deal *will* affect me five years from now. If I was given that promotion, five years from now would look very different."

Diane thinks about this and says, "True. But you don't know how it will all wind up. Maybe losing that sale was what you needed to look inside yourself and become an even better salesperson. And maybe there's an even bigger promotion that you will get because of it -- one that wouldn't have been possible if you had been given that promotion over Julie."

Ben rocks in his desk chair. "I don't know, Diane. I'm all for being positive, but I feel like I'm in the middle of a crisis right now."

"Of course it looks like that now. Just trust me. I'll help you. This will be … a year for reinvention! You helped me get through that break-up last year, let me help you reinvent your sales skills."

Ben is quiet for a few seconds, thinking about what the next year might bring for him. He finally says, "Let's give it a try. What's the worst that can happen?"

Diane raises her eyebrows just as Ben follows up with, "Don't answer that!"

Diane laughs. "The first thing you need to learn how to do is to calm down and not panic. From what you told me, you started to freak out in your MD Anderson meeting when the video wouldn't play."

"If having a full-on panic attack counts as freaking out, then I guess that's fair to say. My heart was pounding, sweat was pouring down my head and the back of my shirt, and I was having trouble catching my breath."

Diane nods. "You were in fight-or-flight. Totally normally. Once you recognize what is happening, you can change course. In that moment, your body is acting as if a saber tooth tiger is chasing you, when, in reality, you are just in a meeting that is tanking. But *you* are safe and not tanking."

"True. I guess I was 'safe.'"

"Yes, I know it can seem like your career is tanking at that moment, but that panic only contributes to a bad situation. You have to learn to stay calm during hard times. I remember when I was taking swimming lessons, my coach always told us to take deep breaths to center ourselves just before we dive in. The key to swimming is breathing, and breathing techniques can really help calm anyone in difficult times. When people get anxious, they tend to take short, shallow breaths. That's the opposite of what we need to be doing."

Ben finds himself subconsciously taking deep breaths as Diane explains this. He has to admit, it does feel good.

"So, how did you get your parents to back off?" Ben asks, bringing the conversation back to Diane.

"They didn't, for a very long time. Their dream was for me to be a doctor, but there was no way that was happening. It was definitely not what I wanted. But once I got into medical technology, I told them that it was *like* being a doctor, because I'm saving lives, too! With technology." She and Ben both laugh at this last part.

"It's true, though!" Ben says. "We are life savers."

"Something like that," Diane responds with a smile before heading to her own cubicle.

Four days later, Ben finds himself in a conference room, holding a paper plate with a piece of yellow cake stacked high. Julie's promotion party.

But not only is it a promotion party for Julie. It feels like a *demotion* party for him. As people congratulate Julie on a job well done, just as many of them come over to say sorry to Ben for losing out.

Ben finds himself getting more and more defensive each time someone looks at him sympathetically and says, "Next time it'll be you, Ben!" His heart is starting to race, and he's sinking back into a corner to avoid his colleagues. He feels his breath quicken, and he starts to panic.

It should be me!, he thinks. *This was* my *time. It should be* my *party. What am I going to do now?*

All the feelings of being not good enough start to resurface, and he thinks about the MD Anderson meeting again. He can feel that familiar anxiety that he felt when the video wouldn't play, and he starts to sweat.

He tells himself he needs to calm down. It's not a good look to have a panic attack at the promotion party of a colleague. A promotion that *he* should have received.

He looks up and sees Diane walk out of the conference room and then remembers what she told him. 5-5-5.

This party is making me anxious. Will this matter in five minutes? Well, yes, not getting the promotion will matter. And I can't leave the party early, either, because that'll look bad, so I'll still be here in five minutes.

Will it matter in five hours? No. I'll be home by then. Watching TV, eating pizza.

'TV and pizza' becomes his mantra, as he slows and controls his breath, like Diane said swimmers do. He breathes deeply, and he actually does start to feel better. Not good enough to take another bite of the sickly-sweet cake on the plate in front of him, but good enough to walk over to his friend Jason who was standing around, drinking a cup of coffee from a small paper cup.

"Ben! I was looking for you," says Jason when Ben approaches.

Great. Another comment about the promotion, he thinks.

But instead, Jason says, "Do you want to go to that new bar downtown tonight? I'm meeting Mike there."

"Sure," Ben replies, relieved. "I'd love to."

A few hours later, Ben walks into the Otopia Roof Top bar, known for its amazing views of downtown Austin around a pool. He sees Jason and Mike saving a stool for him at the bar. They grabbed a corner spot, and Ben slaps Jason on the back before shaking their hands and claiming his seat around the corner next to Mike.

Jason is a brand-new hire at Athena, but he has 9 years of sales experience, and Ben was drawn to him immediately. He is friendly and carefree, and he doesn't take himself too seriously. He's also very good at his job.

Ben doesn't know Mike as well, but Jason befriends everyone, so it's not surprising that the two of them struck up a friendship, despite being in different divisions. Mike works in the Solutions Engineer department with Diane.

"Ben!" Jason exclaims as Ben settles in. "I'm glad you made it. What a week, right?"

"Definitely," Ben replies. "It was a long one."

"Tough break on not getting that promotion, man," Mike says.

Ben shakes his head and tries to get the bartender's attention. "Nah, it is what it is. Julie was the right person for the job. I just have to try harder next time, right?"

Jason and Mike both nod in agreement and fall quiet while Ben orders a beer from the bartender. Ben then turns back to them and continues. "You know Diane? She seems convinced that this was a wake-up call for me to learn new selling strategies and see what else is out there."

"Makes sense," Jason says.

Mike muffles a laugh. "Sounds like some woo-woo stuff to me. 'Always be positive!' 'Live for today!'"

Jason interrupts. "No way, man. A positive mindset is so important. Based on my experience in sales, I've realized that mindset plus preparation plus resilience equals success. I've had almost a decade to figure out what works and what doesn't work for me, and I know that when I don't have the right mindset, I'm not getting the sale."

"I guess," says Mike.

Jason continues, "Think of it like making a cake or something. If you leave out an ingredient, it's just not going to come out good. Same with sales. You need all those ingredients for a good outcome. Each of the steps in this formula is a key ingredient you can use to be successful: mindset, preparation, and resilience."

Jason pauses to take a sip of his beer and then continues. "Think about it. We are always selling ourselves to clients who are considering our product over other companies' products, right? What I say to myself before the call is crucial. If I have the wrong mindset, then the self-talk sounds like, 'I'm not good enough' or 'Why would they pick me?' If I had this mindset, I'd never get hired. So instead, I get myself in the right mindset by remembering other sales I've won and the great outcomes that resulted and telling myself, 'I am confident I can win this sale' and 'I am the right person for this opportunity.'"

By this point, Mike is scrolling through Instagram on his phone and barely listening. But Ben leans in. All he knows is that what he's been doing isn't working, so he's forcing himself to be open to new ideas… including whatever Jason is saying about mindset.

"Okay," Ben replies. "But what about when I'm just not feeling it? Like, if I'm not sure if it will go well, or if I *am* actually the right person?"

"The key to getting into the right mindset is to stack your moments of certainty. It sounds crazy, but I do it before every sales call. I write down three or four times I got a 'yes.' It could be when I got hired, when I got a second date, or when I won an award. Try writing down your moments of certainty. Stack these up in your mind, and on paper, and remember how great you felt. Then put *those* in your head versus fearful thoughts. Try to see the outcome you want to happen before you even start."

"So like visualization?" Ben asks.

"I guess, kind of. Look. What's the worst that can happen if you try? You actually feel good about yourself? That would just be terrible, wouldn't it?" Jason jokes.

Mike finally puts his phone down and says, "I don't know about any of that. But what I do know is that things change. Times change. People change. And the skills that got you there won't keep you there. We all need to learn new skills all the time to stay fresh."

"That's true. I guess we all need to continue improving," Ben says.

"Absolutely," Jason says. "When I was in school, they taught us that whoever speaks first after the closing is the loser. But today, buyers are smart and don't play this tug of war game anymore, if they ever did."

Mike and Ben both nod in agreement.

"But what I've learned," Jason continues, "is that the conversation should actually end with me saying something like, 'So do you want to buy?' and then waiting for an answer. The whole thing is a conversation."

"A conversation?" Mike asks.

"Yes. So that by the end, there's not this big proclamation. It's been back and forth the entire time. There is no loser."

Ben takes a sip of his beer and thinks about his meeting in Houston. Now that he thinks about it, it was a lot of talking *at* them and not *with* them.

"You need to learn to be comfortable with silence." Jason pauses for effect. "Confident people are comfortable with silence. Take some time, let people think about what you just said. Let it sink in. Too many times, I see people jump in just to fill silence, but they are not helping themselves. Just let it sit sometimes. Sometimes, I even think, *I am patient and calm* three times before I speak, rather than thinking *I really need this sale*. People can feel that I'm giving them space to say 'yes' or 'no.'"

The three men sit in silence, smiling at each other to see who will talk first.

Jason laughs and says, "You know what I mean! Let's not make it weird."

The next day, Ben meets his sister Barbara for their weekly bike ride around Zilker Park, which includes the beautiful Barton Springs Pool. His sister is a sound mixer for movies, and her company recently relocated to Austin from Los Angeles, so Barbara moved with her husband Dave and their daughter, Clara. Ben is thrilled to have family nearby.

Ben and Barbara grew up in the suburbs of Chicago, where their parents still live. The Midwest values of showing up and doing what you say you will do have made both of them great friends and employees.

They started this Saturday morning tradition a month ago, and Ben looks forward to it every week: getting outside and getting some exercise, but also catching up with his older sister after living in separate states since college.

On this particular morning, Ben launches into his story of not getting the MD Anderson deal *or* the promotion immediately after they kick off the curb, and after what feels like fifteen minutes of talking and complaining, he finally stops for a breath.

Barbara, to her credit, doesn't rush to fill the silence. Instead, they pedal in peace and quiet for another few minutes before Ben starts again.

"I was just waiting for that promotion to start my life here. As soon as I got that first paycheck with a raise, I was going to apartment hunt and move downtown, and I'd be able to meet someone and go out more. That promotion was the missing piece."

Barbara laughs. Loudly.

"What was that for?" Ben asks, slightly hurt.

"It's just that you're playing that 'as soon as' game. So many of my friends do the same, too. It drives me nuts."

"That 'as soon as' game?" Ben questions.

"Yes," Barbara answers. "*As soon as* this, *as soon as* that. I hear it all the time: 'As soon as I move to California, I'll be happy,' 'As soon as I get married, I'll be happy,' 'As soon as I get in shape, I'll be happy,' 'As soon as I have a new wardrobe, I'll be happy.'"

Ben shakes his head. They are now pedaling over a bridge and towards the lake that surrounds downtown Austin. "You don't get it, Barbara. This is *different*," Ben stresses as they turn the corner.

"It's exactly the same," Barbara responds. "It's important to have positive self-talk. What you say to yourself is more important than what you say to others. Think about it. The person we have the most dialogue with every day is ourselves! When you're present and aware of what you're thinking, it helps you choose between negative or positive thinking. If you're always thinking about what will happen 'as soon as,' how can you really be present in the moment?"

I am *present*, Ben thinks.

"You're not present," Barbara says, as if reading his mind. "Look at what a beautiful day it is. You've barely looked up from your bike, as you ranted about Julie and the promotion. Just enjoy this gorgeous Saturday. You may not live downtown but think about where you *do* live. It's beautiful."

Ben thinks about the nice street he lives on, and the kind couple he rents from. They ride quietly for a moment before Barbara continues. "For example, I have this actor friend who had a part in a hit sitcom and rented a home in Malibu Colony. This was her fantasy, one shared by many other actors. And she was miserable! The script often wasn't funny, and she had to force herself to memorize it. The beach was usually foggy. And worst of all, no one wanted to hear she was unhappy. She had it all—everything everyone in acting strives for. If she wasn't happy, how could anyone be happy?"

Ben is quiet.

"And you have this career fantasy: *As soon as I make over X amount of dollars, I'll be happy.* We all have this magic number in our head we think will make us feel secure. *If I had this amount of money in the bank, then I would feel safe.* It could all go away with one bad investment. What do you think successful people say to that? *So what? I made it once, I can make it again.* But those who don't know the power they have live in fear of losing the money they have. These fear thoughts go away when we take control of the cockpit of our mind with positive thinking. Are you the pilot, or the passenger stuck in the middle seat in the back of the flight of your life?"

"Geez, Barbara. That's a lot."

"I'm just saying: Sometimes it's important to hit the reset button with new knowledge, by being the pilot of our thoughts. We decide how much power to give any one thought. You need to be present to do this."

Ben nods. "The reset button. I like that. It's like what Diane said about reinventing myself."

"Who's Diane?" Barbara asks.

"My co-worker. I've told you about her before. We've been friends for over a year. She's the tech rep for the Lightning Scalpel. She seems to think that I need to learn some more sales skills." Ben pauses. "That's kind of what everyone thinks lately."

"But don't we all need to re-evaluate our lives sometimes? And not in a big, existential way, either. Just checking in with ourselves to make sure that we're on the right track. Benjamin Franklin once wrote, 'He that is good for making excuses is seldom good for anything else.' Can you imagine all the excuses he could have used if he couldn't fly a kite to prove static electricity? *My kite tail is too long, the wind is never right, the key on the end of this is not big enough.* There will *always* be excuses. But when we harness the power of positive thinking and being present, we're giving a gift to others and to ourselves!"

"Why does it feel like everyone is smarter than I am lately?" Ben asked.

"Because they're not you. It's easier said than done," she answers.

They pedal along in silence a bit longer before Barbara adds, "Plus, people love to give advice."

Part 2

On Monday morning, Ben walks into the office with his head a bit higher than last week. He is ready to take on the week, armed with the advice of his friends and family. He spent the rest of the weekend shaking off the non-promotion and gearing himself up to be better. When Ben reminded himself that he is no worse off than he was before the promotion was even a possibility, he quickly pivoted to focus on what he already has versus what he did not get.

And what Ben *has* is a meeting with Dell Senton, another big hospital, next Wednesday.

That gives me over a week to prepare for this and to use what everyone has been teaching me lately to land this sale, he thinks as he settles into his cubicle for the day. *And to figure out how to stop drowning in a sea of sameness, like Carl said.*

Diane appears at his cubicle and hands over Ben's coffee.

"Thanks, Diane. How was your weekend?" Ben asks as he grabs the hot coffee.

"Not bad." Diane responds, leaning against the cubicle entrance. "My mom came to visit, and she stayed over on Saturday, so we just watched old movies and got take-out. What about you?"

"Good," Ben says after taking a sip. "I grabbed drinks with Jason and Mike on Friday after work, and then rode my bike around Barton Springs Pool with my sister on Saturday. And everyone is now a sales expert, apparently."

Diane laughs. "What did they say?"

"Jason was going on about mindset. Kind of like visualization? Like I should picture myself getting the sale. He said I need to be confident going into any pitch meeting."

"Not bad advice," Diane says thoughtfully. "Did he explain just *how* to build confidence?"

"Stacking my moments of certainty," Ben says confidently.

"Huh?" she asks, confused.

"He said that I am supposed to think about three times before where I won sales or got a 'yes' in life. I write them down or remember those and go into sales meetings with those thoughts in my head, rather than the negative self-talk that I apparently have in my head currently."

Diane nods her head slowly as she sips her coffee, and Ben continues.

"Jason said it was important to write down how I felt when I remembered a moment of certainty: proud, happy, strong, whatever. He said that is the key to quiet the monkey mind of negative self talk, like *I'll never get this sale*. We need to replace it with what feeling we want to have before it even happens."

"Right. Like dressing for the job you want, not the job you have," Diane says.

"Exactly! *Think* for the job you want. Or something like that." Ben laughs. "And then he said to be comfortable with silence."

"What does *that* mean?" Diane asks, confused.

"I guess it means to not rush to fill the silence, especially at the end. That sometimes people just need a second to think. And filling silence can make you seem overeager or uncomfortable. He said confident people are comfortable with silence. He even had me practice waiting ten seconds before I answered an objection. He timed me on his iPhone. Trust me, ten seconds can feel like an eternity when you are used to filling in every second."

"Interesting," she responds. "I guess that makes sense. I know when I took public speaking classes in high school, the instructor told us not to fill silence with 'ummm' or 'uhhh' or anything like that. She said it would be better if we just composed our thoughts in silence and then spoke when we were ready."

"Right. And I know for sure that I do that… say 'umm' and stuff while trying to collect my thoughts. Or trying to get a video to play"

"Okay, so two solid pieces of advice. And your sister?"

"Barbara says I'm playing the 'as soon as' game."

"Excuse me?"

"Well, I explained that I was waiting for this promotion to finally move out of the basement and really start the next phase of my life, and she said that it sounded like the 'as soon as' game. You know… 'as soon as I do this, I will be happier, healthier, more successful, whatever.'"

"We all do that sometimes," Diane says.

"Totally. And she went on about how dangerous that can be, which I get. Kind of like: life is going on *right now*. And if we don't live it now, we'll miss it."

"True." Diane takes another sip of her coffee. "But what does that have to do with sales? You said everyone gave sales advice."

"It got me thinking about being present in sales meetings, too," he answers. "And to not think about *When will this meeting end?* or *When will the workday be over?*"

Diane nods her head enthusiastically. "I definitely struggle with that, too, sometimes. I'm always checking my phone for the time when I should be paying attention."

"I think we all do it. And I think that the person you're with can sense when you're not totally there."

"True."

"So, I need to focus on slowing down, being quiet, being present… And being happy and confident where I am right now."

"Sounds like a plan," Diane responds. "A really big plan."

"Agreed. I'm going to prep for my meeting with Dell Senton this week and try to incorporate some of that."

Diane's eyes get wide. "Oh, yes! I forgot you have the Dell Senton meeting coming up. Zack told me."

Zack is the Dell Senton assistant who coordinated the pitch meetings, and he is also a casual acquaintance of Diane and Ben's who lives in Austin.

Ben raises his eyebrows. "You talked to Zack?"

"I ran into him at Starbucks the other day, and he said that Dell Senton was meeting with you and someone else next week before they close Q3."

"Someone else? Did he say who the someone else was?" Ben asks.

"No, but he said she worked for York Surgical."

Ben rolls his eyes and groans. "York Surgical. Great." York Surgical is one of Athena's biggest competitors, and they always seemed to be going head-to-head with each other at these sales meetings.

"I know," Diane responds. "I shouldn't have told you that."

"Why not?"

"Because I know you can suffer from imposter syndrome from time to time."

Ben lets this sink in for a minute.

Do I have imposter syndrome? he thinks. *I definitely struggle with not feeling like I'm good enough… but then I didn't get the promotion, so I wasn't wrong, was I?*

Diane continues. "I think it happens to all of us sometimes. I've seen you get intimidated when you compare yourself to other people instead of focusing on your own progress."

"Focusing on my own progress?" Ben asks, unsure.

"Yes. For example, I remember one time I was swimming in a competition in college. I beat this other girl, the best one in the group, by just half of a second. When I ran over to my coach, he told me that the girl turned her head quickly to look at me while she was swimming, and that cost her the race. If she was just focused on her own progress, like I was, she most likely would have beaten me."

Ben drinks his coffee and thinks about his own athletic career, which was pretty much nonexistent. He did join the track team in high school, as an alternative to all of the contact sports his friends were playing. But he wasn't very good. And Diane was right; he did constantly compare himself to the other guys on the team. Even when he beat his own personal record, he never celebrated because it still wasn't as good as his best friend, Charlie.

He considers what Diane is saying about focusing on his own progress. Finally, Ben says, "I guess that's easy for you to say, though. You're so talented. You know all about the technology and mechanics of these devices. You're smart *and* athletic *and* calm."

"Yes, yes, all true…" Diane jokes. "But don't forget that it's your *soft skills* that make you stronger."

"Soft skills?" Ben looks at her dubiously. "Like what?"

"Well, like empathy and listening and storytelling," she answers, counting them off her fingers.

Ben laughs and rolls his eyes. "Right. Like empathy and storytelling will really make me a great salesperson."

"Of course they will!" she exclaims. "How do you think Julie got the promotion?"

"By making more sales?" Ben responds.

"Right. And she made more sales because she leveraged her soft skills. In general, people don't take soft skills as seriously as hard skills. People don't think they're as important. They think that hard skills are the most important thing that someone needs to do a job well. Think about it: If you're an architect, your hard skills are what you learned in school, like how to design a building. If you're a lawyer, your hard skills are what you learned in law school and what you studied to pass the bar. If you're a keynote speaker, your hard skills are knowing how to put together a talk that has a beginning, middle, and end."

Ben thinks about this as he swivels in his desk chair. He realizes that he does this himself. He has always considered hard skills to be more important than soft skills, especially in a career.

Diane continues. "But no matter what your profession, mastering the soft skills is what makes you stronger than your competition. The old way of winning new business is to just show the product and hope that would be enough to get a sale. But it's not like that anymore. People buy from someone they *like*."

"I guess so," Ben says skeptically.

"Enter: soft skills! One of the best ways to increase your likeability is to show empathy. The more people think you understand the stress they are under and how you can help them, the more they like and want to work with you. Telling stories is a great way to build rapport, especially when you tell a story about what inspired you to do what you do. People love working with people who are passionate because that usually means the process will be fun."

"That actually makes sense. Who wants to work with people they don't like?" Ben feels like he is starting to understand where Diane is coming from.

"I suggest investing some time in training yourself to practice listening and empathy. When you do that, your soft skills will become stronger—just like your physical workouts."

Ben looks incredulous. "How? How do you know all of this?"

Diane laughs and finishes her last sip of coffee before tossing the empty cup in the trash in Ben's cubicle. "I'm just a genius. And athletic, and smart… anything else?"

Ben laughs. "Thanks a lot for that. I've definitely thought about being a likeable, empathic person, of course, but I never actually considered how important that might be in sales calls."

"Absolutely. Wouldn't *you* rather give your business to someone you like?"

"Yes. I guess I would. That's true," Ben says.

"Of course. And *that's* how you distinguish yourself from your competition. Be more likeable, more empathetic, more trusting. Make it about more than just the sale."

"Makes sense to me," Ben nods, thinking.

"You got it. Now get to work, already."

"Yes ma'am," Ben grins, and turns around to get started.

Part 3

Two days later, Ben is again sitting in his cubicle when he hears Diane call, "Hey, Ben!"

He turns around and sees her approach, and she stops to stand just outside.

"Hey, Diane. How was lunch?"

"Good. Just grabbed sushi from the cafeteria."

"Yuck. Cafeteria sushi?" Ben makes a face.

Diane laughs. "It's really good, actually. Our building's best-kept secret!"

"I doubt that."

"Why are you in such a bad mood?" Diane teases.

Ben sighs. "Sorry. I'm not. Just worried about the meeting next week."

"I know. Do you want to run anything by me? The offer still stands for me to listen to your pitch."

"I'm still working on it. Trying to prepare."

Diane says, "A friend of mine on Instagram just posted a quote by Arthur Ashe, the famous tennis player. He said, 'One important key to success is self-confidence. An important key to self-confidence is preparation.'"

"How motivational," Ben deadpans.

"Ha! I think it's really helpful to think about. You talked about stacking your moments of certainty to be confident the other day, and that absolutely can help. But the *real* thing that will make you confident is being totally prepared. You can walk in there knowing that you *got this*. And the best way to prepare is to practice."

"You mean, make sure all videos are working properly?" he jokes.

"Well. That, too. But *practice*. I read an article about the preparation that Emma Boettcher did to beat the *Jeopardy!* champion James Holzhauer, which was so impressive. She actually wrote a paper in graduate school about whether certain clues could predict how hard the question was. After she'd been called to appear on the show, she prepared by watching it every day and pretending the pen in her hand was her clicker to buzz in. Then she decided that wasn't realistic enough and used a toilet paper holder as her pretend buzzer. She had to beat the odds of winning against Holzhauer, and she did it by preparation."

"Wow, that really is interesting. I loved that guy."

"To prepare yourself for success at a sales pitch, an interview, or presentation, you could write down three questions you think you'll be asked and be prepared to answer them before they ask you," Diane offers.

"Oh, I like that," Ben responds. "Anticipate the questions. That's a great idea."

Diane looks pleased. "Another way to help you prepare to get your confidence up and learn to think on your feet is doing what they do in the improv world. Improv is all about saying, 'Yes, and …' instead of 'No.' When you practice taking what's thrown at you and responding in a way that keeps the conversation going, you'll be able to trust yourself to come up with a good answer on the spot."

"Oh, I've heard of that in improv. Like, you're supposed to say 'Yes and' to whatever the other person does or says instead of going against it."

"Exactly," Diane says.

"That's helpful. Thanks."

"No problem."

"I'm going to get back to it. Are you around later so I can run the pitch by you?"

"Yes, sure. I have a three o'clock meeting with my boss Uma, but I can do 4?"

"That works. I'm going to reserve a conference room. I'll email you."

"Sounds good. See you later," Diane says, and she walks away towards her own cubicle on the other side of the building.

Ben turns back around in his chair and stares at the computer, thinking about what Diane just said about preparation. He thought he was prepared for all of his pitches, but it seems that apparently, he was preparing the wrong information.

What can I do to get clients interested in what I'm saying? Ben wonders. *Maybe if I know more about them, I can better understand what they are looking for.*

He Googles "Dell Senton Medical Center" on his phone. He has been on their website a dozen times, but this time, his search pulls up their Instagram page. After scrolling through their feed a bit, he is struck by how clearly the company values their employees. They had an ice cream social last month in the parking lot to celebrate the end of summer, for example. A few posts down, he sees that a bunch of employees recently ran a 5K to raise money for breast cancer awareness.

Ben remembers when his mother was diagnosed with breast cancer fifteen years ago. It came as such a shock to everyone in his family, and the year after that was mostly a blur of doctor appointments and chemo and wigs and fear. His father was a wreck, and his mother was so sick. He and Barbara really had to step up, making dinners and running errands. It was a hard time for the whole family.

He's lost in thought when he hears a booming voice behind him. "Planning on working at all today?"

Ben jolts up, realizing what it looks like: that he is staring off into space, while mindlessly scrolling Instagram.

He turns around, hoping that he misheard the voice.

But no, there's Carl, looming over him, pointing at the phone.

"I just thought," Carl goes on loudly, "that the week before your meeting with Dell Senton, you might be doing something other than looking at pictures of dogs on your phone."

Ben looks down to see that he is, in fact, looking at pictures of dogs. From a pet adoption program where the Dell Senton employees volunteered over the summer.

"Sorry, Carl," Ben says, putting his phone down on his desk. "I was just researching Dell Senton to see if I can learn anything about them before our meeting next week."

"And you found dogs?!" Carl bellows.

"Apparently," Ben responds, feeling too little to stand up for himself.

Carl is quiet for just long enough to make Ben feel like a small child who just disappointed his father. "I just came by to remind you how important this meeting is next week."

Ben nods, eyes on his feet.

Carl continues. "I can't go with you this time. I know you're probably thrilled."

Ben tries hard not to make a single move that could be taken for affirmation.

"But I really need you to land this sale. It's important to the company, it's important to me, and it's important to you."

Point taken, Ben thinks. He says, "Of course. Absolutely. I'm prepared."

"Right," Carl replies, glancing again at the cell phone on the desk. He looks up to meet Ben's eyes, and the silence sits between them like a thick fog. Ben forces himself to keep Carl's gaze, rather than to look away or fill the silence with an awkward laugh. Finally, Carl turns and walks away from Ben's cubicle without another word.

Ben works through lunch, memorizing (again) everything he can about the Lightning Scalpel. Of course, he is thinking about what Diane said about soft skills, but surely the facts are important, too, right?

At three o'clock, Ben remembers his meeting with Diane and quickly reserves a conference room down the hall. He emails Diane:

Hey!

Thanks again for offering to hear the pitch. I reserved room 504 for 4:00 p.m.

Ben spends the next few minutes scrolling through his Instagram a bit - hey, he didn't take lunch! - and finds himself once again looking through Dell Senton's feed. He thinks about what Diane said about having empathy. *Maybe I could talk about my mother's breast cancer? Make some sort of connection to their charitable work and their company's values? Will that make me likable… or pathetic?*

He then remembers reading Tim Sanders' book *The Likeability Factor*, which includes research that shows doctors spend more time with patients they like. It makes sense to him: showing empathy and vulnerability makes you authentic and more likable. That sounds a lot like what Diane was saying about soft skills making you stronger. Sharing his own personal story is relevant to the Dell Senton culture, and maybe it will make him more relatable and authentic.

He decides to run the idea by Diane at their meeting. He then spends the rest of the time making sure the video plays, now that he uploaded it directly to the presentation. No Internet needed.

Four o'clock comes, and Ben takes the short walk to room 504, where Diane is sitting, checking her cell phone.

"Hey, Diane," Ben says on his way in. "Thanks again for meeting with me. This'll be quick."

"Hey! No need to be quick. I'm avoiding Julie anyway. She wants to talk about new product features, and I can't handle another meeting that could've been an email."

Ben laughs. "I know all about that. I'm much more of an email person myself, too." He pauses for a beat. "And now that I think about it, maybe that's not the best thing for a salesperson to say." He flushes and looks at Diane for encouragement.

"Nonsense," Diane responds. "You can't let this whole thing get you down. You got to where you are today because you are passionate about your job and you know your products like the back of your hand. You just need to brush up those soft skills, and you'll be back and better than ever."

Ben sits in the chair across from Diane and opens his laptop on the table in front of him. "Thanks. Speaking of soft skills, I noticed that Dell Senton participates in a ton of charity work. I actually thought I'd start by mentioning how much I respect that about them. You know, after what my mom went through, I think anything that anyone can do to raise awareness for causes like cancer is amazing."

Diane nods approvingly. "That's awesome. I think that's a great way to build a connection."

Ben peers at her. "Are you sure? Not too personal? Too much? I'm not looking for a handout here."

Diane laughs. "I'm sure. No one is going to give you a sale just because your mom had breast cancer anyway. Especially once they find out that she is currently on a golf vacation in La Jolla."

Ben starts laughing at the thought of his mom. Diane's right. She's probably bragging to her friends about her improved golf score.

"And also, it's a good time to connect the Dell Senton values to the Athena values," Diane continues.

"I'm listening…" Ben leans forward in his seat.

"Uma and I were just talking about a way to incorporate Athena's company values into our products and sales, and what you said about Dell Senton's company values made me think about making those connections across industries. For instance, one of our core values is also charity."

"That's right," Ben says, remembering. "I know we do charity work, too, like collecting food products at Thanksgiving and Toys for Tots in December."

"Exactly," Diane says. "Maybe once you talk about yourself in the opening, you can then make a connection to Athena's values. Don't be afraid to talk about how proud you are to work for a company that gives back, and maybe say that you imagine the people at Dell Senton feel the same way."

"That's a great idea. Okay, so that's the plan. I'll make a small connection to myself, then discuss Athena on a larger scale, and then move on to the product."

"Yes," Diane replies. "But when you move on, don't forget that connection in the beginning. You really want to foster it and make them *like* you."

"See, this is what I'm talking about!" Ben responds. "I've never worried about them *liking* me. As long as they *like* the product, then I assumed everything would be okay."

"That's what I've been trying to tell you: not anymore. Things are different," Diane says. "Listen, people usually give three yeses and then a no."

Diane stands and walks over to the dry erase board at the front of the room and picks up the purple marker. She writes:

We like the idea.
We like the product.
We think this might work.

Then she picks up the red marker and writes underneath:

We want to think about it.

She turns to Ben and says, "That's the no. The first three yeses are built on logic, but to get the last yes, you need to use *emotion*. You need all four yeses to make a sale, right? The fourth one comes when there is an emotional connection."

Ben cocks his head to the side, re-reading the board and trying to catch up to Diane's thought process.

Diane continues. "I have a friend, John Bates, who worked with NASA executives. He said that he determined that the last criteria people have to pass to become an astronaut is: 'Are you likeable?'"

"To be an astronaut? Who the heck cares if the person is likeable or not?"

"Well, to start, probably the other astronauts who will spend the next months or so crammed in a tin can with him."

Ben laughs. "Yes, I suppose that's true."

"But really," Diane says. "When you're being interviewed in any position, including a sales call, people are thinking, 'Are you the kind of person I'd want to have over to my home for dinner?'"

"You think so?"

"Absolutely!"

Ben is quiet for a moment, considering this. Were people really wondering if he was likable? Is that what those two junior executives at MD Anderson were thinking about as he fumbled around with the video? He's not totally sold yet, and he explains this to Diane.

"I don't know. I'm trying to wrap my head around this, but I'm finding it hard to believe that the people I'm selling to are thinking about what it's like to have dinner with me."

Diane sighs and sits back down in the chair across from Ben. "Think about this. Remember when Carl used to give those speeches at our annual team meetings? And he would always say," and here, Diane puts on her best Carl voice, as deep and condescending as she can go, "*'Remember, everyone! To win the sale, you'll need to get people to know, like, and trust you!'*"

Ben cringes at the memory. "Yes, I remember. Know, like, trust. Like a drill sergeant."

"Well consider flipping that around," Diane says. "Rather than people thinking with their head then their heart then their gut, people really do the opposite."

"Hmm," Ben says. "Go on."

"People make decisions with their gut first. *Then* their heart. *Then* their head."

"So rather than know, like, trust, it's really trust, like, know?" Ben asks.

"Exactly!" Diane exclaims. "People will decide quickly if they trust you, then decide if they like you, before they use their head to decide if they know you and your product, and, ultimately, if they are going to buy from you. Many people think that if they give out enough information about how many successful placements they have made or all the benefits that come with a device, that people will suddenly want to take action. The mistake is thinking if you get people to know you and the offering, they will then like you and eventually trust you."

"Wow. See, I totally understand that because I do it, too. I trust my gut first when meeting someone. Not my head, necessarily."

"You got it! The order was all wrong. People have to first trust you, which is a gut thing. In fact, the handshake came about to show you didn't have a gun in your hand. Did you know that?"

Ben shakes his head, and Diane continues. "Then it moves to the heart, where people decide if they like you or not. Then it moves to the head where people think *Can I see myself working with you?* Once you know to start from the gut and work your way to the heart and then the head, you will handle the trust issue."

"How so?" Ben asks.

"In sales, when you are honest with your clients, and you give them a fair rate, they will learn to trust you. Over time, you get more referrals, because you're viewed as someone who is a straight-shooter, as someone who understands that good deals mean both sides walk away from the table with smiles on their faces. Clients buy from you even when you don't have the best rates, because they trust you, and you treat them with respect and honesty. And then you're going to take it to another level when talking about Athena's values, which will allow the client to *like* and *trust* the entire company, as well."

"Really interesting." Ben says, really thinking about everything that Diane has been explaining. "This is all very helpful. Thanks for that."

"No problem."

Ben looks at his watch. "It looks like we have 30 minutes left. I really appreciate all of this, but would you mind if we went over some specs and stats of the Lightning Scalpel again? I just want to make sure I have it all down. And I also want to test the video in here," Ben says, pulling up his presentation on his laptop.

"Sure thing," Diane says.

After meeting with Diane, Ben heads home and thinks about all the new things he's been learning lately. He thinks about building likeability and sharing his knowledge, after starting with trust. He thinks about ways to show respect and honesty to clients to build their respect towards him.

He spends the rest of the week preparing for his Dell Senton pitch and going over the numbers and information again and again. He has practiced his opener, where he'll mention how much he values their charity work and talk a bit about his mom, although he's still not entirely sure that a sales rep talking about his mother during a pitch is necessarily a good thing. And then he works on discussing the company and how Dell Senton and Athena both have similar core values. It's not his usual pitch opener, but he is excited to try it out.

Part 4

Ben's meeting with Dell Senton was two days ago, and he feels confident walking into work Friday morning. He runs the meeting through his head for what feels like the millionth time while he waits for the elevator up to the fifth floor.

Before his meeting, he took Jason's advice and stacked his own moments of certainty. He even wrote them down on a Post-It and stuck them inside the notebook he brought to the meeting. In the meeting itself, Ben took Diane's advice, even though it seemed like a risk. Instead of the usual boring corporate opening ("Thanks for this opportunity. I'm excited to be here."), he opened it with his personal story about what he and his family went through when his mom was diagnosed with cancer. He then talked about their Instagram post and commented on the 5K run they did to raise funds for breast cancer research.

He said that so often, people forget the values and purpose of why they are all in healthcare in the first place. But seeing Dell Senton encourage employees to do something on their own time, like raising money for breast cancer, touched Ben.

Ben went on to say that Athena values charity and making a difference, and he mentioned a few charity events that he himself had participated in. He then explained that Athena and Dell Senton both shared those core company values.

And it did seem to work. He was able to make a connection, and the vulnerable, candid, and personal pitch opening took the buyers by surprise. As a result, instead of having their defenses up as they normally did when they heard a pitch, hearing a personal story that resonated with their company's values seemed to immediately allow them to see Ben as a person and not just another rep pitching them.

In fact, one of the purchasing people in the meeting said that he'd heard hundreds of pitches over the years and most of them are forgettable, but he would remember Ben's pitch for a long time.

Ben went a bit out of his comfort zone, for sure, talking about his mother, but the executive really seemed to appreciate his recognition of their charitable work. She even mentioned her own father's battle with prostate cancer, and they bonded a bit over that.

Just as the elevator *dings* and the doors open to take Ben up, Diane walks through the front door. "You look deep in thought," she says.

"Hey, Diane!" Ben turns to greet her. "I was just thinking about the Dell Senton meeting last week."

"I'm sure you are." Diane smiles at him and waves her arm to let him get on the elevator first.

"How was your night? Do anything fun?" Ben asks as the doors close behind him.

"Actually, I finally got all caught up with *Ted Lasso*. I was a few episodes behind, and I feel like that's all anyone's been talking about lately."

"Oh yes!" Ben responds. "I saw the first episode, but I never really got into it. How is it?"

"I think it's great," Diane says. "There was a scene last night where Ted was playing darts with some guy in a pub, and the guy totally thought Ted would be terrible at it, so they made a bet. But it turns out, Ted is a great darts player, and he winds up winning. And just as he's winning, he tells a story about a Walt Whitman quote he saw that said, *'Be curious, not judgmental.'"*

"Oh really?" Ben asks, only semi-interested.

"Yes," Diane continues, as the elevator doors open at the fifth floor. They both turn left and start walking toward Ben's cubicle, and Diane continues as they walk.

"Ted explains how he was bullied growing up, and he realized after reading that quote that the bullies were being judgmental, so it wasn't even about him at all. And if they were curious and asked questions, they would get to know him instead of writing him off."

"Nice. So, I suppose there's a lesson in there somewhere for me?" Ben jokes.

Diane laughs. "Well, I'm just saying… maybe if you were more curious about your clients, and asked them questions about themselves, it would help!"

"Ask them questions? So, what, I'm talking about the Lightning Scalpel and then stop and say, *'Hey, Joe, what's your favorite color?'*"

Diane rolls her eyes and lets out a sigh as they turn the corner to his cubicle.

"Not exactly like that, no. More like… asking them why they got into the medical industry, what makes them passionate about medical tools, what would help them to best do their job? And then you, and our whole company, can really use that information. In fact, learning more about *everyone* can really improve our company."

Ben slides his backpack off his shoulders and lets it fall to the floor next to his chair. He sits down and swivels to turn his computer on, and then turns back to Diane, who stands at the entrance of the cubicle, leaning against the wall like usual. She's not finished with this idea.

"If we knew more about everyone and what got them here and what makes them passionate about their jobs, we could use all that to create stories and really start to make connections with our clients."

"Stories?"

"Stories. Listen, I have to get to work. You know, some of us have real jobs around here," she jokes.

Ben rolls his eyes and turns back to the computer. "Have a nice day. I'll talk to you later."

"Bye!" Diane calls out as she walks away.

Ben opens his Slack, and sees a message from Julie, sent 45 minutes ago. *The early bird gets the worm and all that, I suppose*, Ben thinks.

@Ben, I sent you a calendar invite for 10a.m. Can you come by for a chat?

A chat, Ben thinks. *Great.*

He Slacks her back: *Sure thing, @Julie.*

He finds the invite in his inbox and clicks "Accept," hoping that Julie isn't judging him for not clicking it sooner.

At 9:55 on the dot, Ben knocks on Julie's office door, which is slightly ajar.

"Hi, Ben!" Julie calls from inside, and Ben pushes the door open to find her sitting behind a glass-topped desk, with two big monitors in front of her. She has her glasses perched at the end of her nose, while she seems engrossed with something on the screen. She looks up and smiles and waves Ben into one of the two big leather chairs in front of the desk but then quickly goes back to whatever it is she's reading on the computer.

After what feels like an eternity but is closer to 45 seconds, Julie snaps her glasses off her face and stands up to look at Ben.

"Hey, Ben!"

"Hi, Julie! Nice to see you."

"Thanks for coming by," she says, as she moves out from behind the desk and closes the door on her way to sit in the other leather chair, next to Ben.

"Of course. Happy to see you in this nice office and out of a cubicle."

Julie laughs quickly and looks around her. "Yes, perk of the job, I guess." They are both quiet, while the elephant in the room settles. (*This could have been my office*, Ben thinks.)

Julie breaks the silence. "Listen, I just want to start by saying that I have always respected you and your work. I was just as surprised as you were when I got that promotion, trust me. You really took me under your wing when I started here, and I will never forget that."

"Don't mention it," Ben says, waving his hand in the air. "You were clearly the best one for the job. You deserve it."

"Yes, well. Thanks."

"Sure."

"Anyway, I did have something else I wanted to talk about today, too. I got a call from Dell Senton. They're going to pass."

"*Pass?!* You're kidding me!" Ben lets his emotions get the best of him. "Afraid not. They said they really liked you and thought you were kind and personable, but they just don't feel a need for our Lightning Scalpel right now."

Ben's face turns red. "But that's impossible! How could they not need it? Every doctor needs it!"

"Well, I know that, and you know that. But they weren't convinced."

"I absolutely cannot believe this," Ben says, throwing his hands in the air. "I worked so hard on that presentation. I did my research. I *knew* them, and I *knew* the product."

"I'm not doubting any of that," Julie responds calmly.

"I don't know how this happened," Ben says, and hangs his head, looking at his feet.

"I know this isn't the news you wanted… *any* of us wanted. But I wanted to tell you myself, before Carl gets to you."

At the mention of the name, Ben's stomach turns. "Ugh.. Carl. He is going to be *so mad*."

"Yes, he probably will," Julie says sympathetically. "But what are you going to do about it?"

"What do you mean?" Ben asks, still staring at his shoes.

"I mean, rejection stings. But it's also part of the job. The most important thing to do now is to bounce back."

"Bounce back? My job is in serious jeopardy. How do I bounce back from that?"

"Well, I don't know if it's in *serious* jeopardy. It's a setback, sure, but the client really did like you, and they invited you to come back and pitch again in the next quarter. So, there's that."

Ben stays quiet.

Julie continues. "Listen, it's important to be resilient. Do you get up quickly after you fall? My brother is a real estate agent, and he once told me that the number one difference between the top one percent of agents and those who struggle to make a living is how fast they bounce back after getting a *no*. The top one percent let it go immediately. The others *say* they let it go, but many of them mope around in a bad mood for two weeks or more."

"You really believe that?" Ben asks, finally looking up and catching Julie's eye.

"I really do," she responds.

Ben sighs and sits back in the seat a little further.

Julie goes on. "In business and in life, it's not a question of *whether* you'll get knocked down, but *when* you'll get knocked down. And then how fast you'll get back up. My key to resilience is to never take rejection personally. When I miss out on a sale, I tell myself, 'A *no* now, doesn't mean *no forever.*'"

Ben nods, still feeling the Dell Senton rejection in his gut.

"And it's true!" Julie says. "Just look: Dell Senton wants to speak to you again. So, it's really *not* a *no forever.*"

"Thanks," Ben mumbles. "So now I just need to bounce back, huh?"

"Yep!" says Julie, a little too enthusiastically. "To become more resilient, see how fast you can let rejection go. Don't go crazy talking about it with friends and co-workers or complain about 'how tough it is out there.'"

"Right." Ben says, because he can't think of anything else to say at the moment.

"Have you ever heard of Bonnie St. John?" she asks.

Ben shakes his head.

"I saw a TEDx talk that she gave on resilience. Her right leg had to be amputated below the knee when she was five years old, and she went on to compete in the U.S. Paralympic Ski Team with a prosthetic leg."

"Wow," Ben says, impressed.

Diane goes on, "The event took the combined time of two different races. In the first race, she came in first place. In the second race, the mountain had more ice on it, and everyone was falling. Bonnie fell, too, but she finished the event. They told her she came in second place overall. While she was the fastest going down on the first race, she was not the fastest getting back up after the fall on the second race."

"Oh man. That must've been tough."

"The point is: How fast we get back up is the key to success! Unlike sports, sales does not give a medal or reward for coming in second place. Nobody wins *every* sale, but those who get back up fast are the ones who meet their goals."

Ben sits quietly, thinking about how quickly he can get back up from this rejection.

"Anyway," Julie says, standing up, signaling the end of the meeting. "You'll be fine. Let me know if I can do anything."

Ben stands up, too. "Thanks, Julie. You, uhh, too. Let me know if you need anything."

Julie smiles in a way that Ben can't quite figure out and heads back behind her desk, leaving Ben to let himself out.

When he gets back to his desk, he shoots Diane a text. *Free for lunch? I'll buy you some gross cafeteria sushi.*

His phone dings with a response: *Who can turn down an offer like that? I'll be by your cube at 12:15.*

It's not until Diane and Ben are sitting across from each other in the cafeteria, food in front of them, next to a massive wall of windows looking over the green grass in the back of the building, that Ben says, "So. Dell Senton didn't work out."

Diane's eyes open wide. "Nooo!" She whisper-yells.

"Yes. I know."

"I can't believe it. You were so ready for that meeting," Diane says in disbelief.

"I know. I told Julie the same thing."

"Julie?" she asks.

"She broke the news to me this morning."

"That must've hurt."

"It definitely didn't feel good," Ben says.

"I'm so sorry, Ben. I thought this was going to be the turning point."

"So did I. But Julie did say that they want me to come back next quarter, so maybe a little silver lining?" Ben offers.

"Well, that's something! It's not a *no forever*."

"Julie said the same thing."

Diane maneuvers her chopsticks to grab a piece of her spicy tuna roll. It's an art, really, the way she adds just a bit of wasabi, before dipping the whole thing in soy sauce.

Mouth still half-full, Diane asks, "So where do you think it went wrong?"

"You really don't beat around the bush, do you?" Ben takes a bit of his own turkey and Swiss sandwich to take a bite.

"No point," Diane says. "We need to figure this out."

They sit in friendly silence for a bit, each eating their lunches.

"Are you terrified to fail?" Diane asks.

"Whoa," Ben says, putting his sandwich down. "Coming in hard with the questions today, don't you think?"

"I mean it! For instance, I'm terrified of public speaking. Research shows that many people have a fear of public speaking. Turns out, there's even a word for it: glossophobia."

"Glossophobia," Ben tries the word out.

"My friend Steve Rohr wrote a book about it called *Scared Speechless*. When I talked to him about it, he said that this fear is instinctual. When we are in front of other people, we are separated from the herd, and we fear being attacked."
"Attacked? Really?"

"It's true! It's our animal instinct. We need to teach ourselves to break through the terror barrier."

"The terror barrier?"

"Yep. When you break down the barrier, you let go of the real fear, which is the fear of rejection."

"And what causes the fear of getting rejected?" Ben asks between bites.

"Well, when we get a *no*, we think it means *no forever*, like Julie said. But what if it just means *no for now*?"

Ben thinks about this, as Diane continues. "When we get rejected, we start to reject ourselves and what we are selling. What if we reframe that to 'I never reject myself or doubt my abilities. no matter what the outcome'?"

"Easier said than done," Ben says.

"Oh absolutely! But there are solutions to any fear."

"And this is the part where you tell me what those are?" Ben asks.

"Precisely," Diane retorts. "No matter what terrifies you, here are the three solutions to any fear. First of all, remember that you control your thoughts. You are the thinker thinking the thoughts. When you feel fear in your body, ask yourself, *What if I am just excited, versus scared?* They feel very similar; we can rename it."

Ben thinks for a moment. "So, you want me to tell myself I'm excited for a sales pitch?"

"Yes. I do. Then, second of all, tell yourself you are enough, and what you have to offer is valuable. Instead of being intimidated to reach out or pitch to someone new, tell yourself you are doing them a favor. This is their lucky day to be hearing from me."

Ben laughs. "Their lucky day to be hearing from *me*?!"

"Well, yes! You have a lot to offer, don't forget. Your job is to *help them make their job easier.*"

"I guess when you put it that way… that really is what we're doing, making their job easier. Okay, what's the third?"

"The third solution to fear is to remember that what other people think about you is none of your business! Let go of having to be a perfectionist at anything. Instead, think of yourself as a progressionist who celebrates his own progress."

"A progressionist? I like that," Ben says.

"Perfectionism doesn't exist, and it can be dangerous to try to be perfect. Instead, think about your own progress," Diane says. "When your identity is so strong that the results don't make you go up and down the self-esteem roller coaster, you are free to overcome any fear that has been holding you back. The next time you feel any form of fear, just tell yourself *I'm safe and fearless.*"

"I'm safe and fearless," Ben repeats.

"Right. When you focus on your own progress, you win!"

"Just like that story you told me about your swim meet. About the girl who looked to see how you were doing and then lost?"

"Exactly." Diane seems happy with herself, as she eats the last piece of sushi, wipes her face, and crumbles her napkin into her dish.

"It's just…" Ben starts. "I really thought that by opening up with my mom's breast cancer and building trust with that personal story, I would have made a connection."

"While you may have gotten the potential buyers to *trust* and *like* you with that story, you probably still did not answer the unspoken question everyone has which is *Will this work for me?*"

"What do you mean?" Ben asks.

"*Will this work for me?* That's what everyone really needs to know, right?"

"And how do I answer that for them?" Ben asks.

Diane is quiet for a moment and then asks, "Have you ever used case stories in your pitches?"

"Case studies? Yes, sure."

"No, not case studies. Case *stories*," she emphasizes.

"Diane, you're going to have to be a bit more clear here."

Diane laughs. "A case story is different from a case study in that you tell it in such a way that people see themselves in the story. It's not a case study about *other* people, but a case *story* that allows the buyer to put themselves in their place. This is the secret: It's not enough just to tell a story. It must be a story that the people see themselves in."

"Ooo-kay," Ben says slowly. "Tell me more."

"No can do. I have to get back to work. What's your plan for this weekend?"

"The usual: Bike ride with Barbara Saturday morning. Trying to get my mom on the phone to see how the golf match went. Oh, and meeting Jason on Sunday for a run."

"A run?" Diane teases.

"Yes! I run sometimes!"

"If you say so."

Ben stands up and grabs his trash. As he and Diane walk towards the door, he asks, "Do you want to grab a coffee on Saturday afternoon? Are you around? I could really use some more advice. And now you really piqued my interest with the case story stuff."

"Sure, that sounds good. I'll meet you at Mozart's Cafe at two o'clock? The one on the lake?"

"Awesome. See you there."

"Bye!" Diane calls out as she takes a right, towards the conference rooms and her next meeting.

Part 5

At two o'clock on Saturday, Ben sits outside at Mozart's Cafe basking in the early autumn sun and overlooking Lake Austin. His phone dings with a text from Diane.

Running ten mins late sry

No worries, Ben texts back.

He opens Facebook on his phone and sees that his mom posted some pictures from her golf game, so he scrolls through them for the next minute before looking up and taking in the view. *Be present*, Barbara's voice echoes in his mind. Ben looks over and sees people sitting on the dock. He looks over the lake at the ducks and turtles and sees the hills beyond. It doesn't really feel like he's in Texas at all.

Who needs an ocean when you have a lake and hills like this? he thinks, enjoying being in the moment.

Ben hears Diane calling his name as she approaches the table.

"Hi!" she calls and dumps her handbag on the table with a sigh. "Sorry about that. Traffic."

"No problem," Ben replies. "I hate traffic."

"Ha! I don't know many people who *like* traffic," Diane responds as she sinks into the chair across from him.

"True," Ben says. "But one time, I was sitting in traffic trying to get to a sales call. You know that feeling when you're going to be late for something important? I felt sick to my stomach… like I had no control! My heart was racing, and I started to sweat. I still have nightmares about it. But I finally had to remind myself that being late is better than getting into an accident, right? If I'm late, I can always reschedule or shorten my pitch."

Diane grins widely.

"What?" asks Ben.

"Just… that was a really great story. I felt myself in that situation. *That's* what I'm talking about!" Diane replies.

"I have no idea what you're talking about," he says. "Coffee?"

"Yes, please. Black. Hot."

Ben nods and heads inside to grab their coffees. There are two people in line in front of him, which gives him just enough time to decide to get a piece of coffee cake and a chocolate chip scone, too, for good measure.

He heads back out with the two coffees and bag of pastries and sits across from Diane.

"Thanks," Diane says as she reaches for the cup. "Coffee cake?" she asks, pointing to the bag.

"You know it. And a scone."

"Perfect!"

Ben and Diane get settled and dig into the pastries while they catch each other up on their lives a bit. Ben talks about his bike ride with his sister Barbara this morning. Barbara and her husband, Dave, are going to a concert tonight, and Ben offered to babysit his niece, Clara.

"Hmm," Diane says. "I don't picture you as a babysitter."

"No, not really. This is actually my first time. When Clara was younger, I couldn't figure out all that bottle and diaper stuff, but she's five now, so I figure it's safer." Ben says and laughs.

After the coffee cake is gone and there is just a bit of scone left, Ben finally says. "Okay. Let's get to it. Case stories."

"Case stories." Diane says in response, putting down her coffee as if a signal to begin official business.

"You think this is the missing piece?" Ben asks.

"I really do. So many salespeople don't even try to tell a story, and then they wonder why they keep coming in second place. And those who *do* tell a story often make the same mistakes: they make *themselves* the hero of the story. Or else the stories become so long and complicated, no one can remember it… let alone repeat it. Or the stories are incredibly boring, without any emotion. You need high stakes in the story to get people to care."

"Don't be the hero. Don't be complicated. Don't be boring." Ben recalls. "Got it."

"It's not that simple!" Diane laughs. "Remember the three Cs. Your story needs to be clear, concise, and compelling. It needs to be clear because the confused mind always says *no*, but no one will tell you they're confused. Your story needs to be concise so that people can remember and repeat the story for the meeting after the meeting."

"The meeting after the meeting?"

"Yep. Your sales meeting is the first one. After they hear you pitch, and your competitors', there is another meeting without any reps in the room. That's when they have a conversation about what everybody thinks and who they recommend. And if no one's told a memorable story, then you're all stuck in that sea of sameness that Carl was talking about. They say, *They all sound the same; let's just go with the cheapest price.*"

Ben nods his head in painful recognition.

"But if you told a story that they can repeat, sometimes even to upper-level executives who didn't hear any of the pitches, they become your brand ambassadors. The second meeting is when the people you pitched to talk about you and the product. And if you tell a concise story, they are more likely to remember that story and be able to repeat it at the meeting after the meeting. What they might *not* remember are the numbers that you threw at them."

"That makes a lot of sense," Ben says. "They need something to remember you by, and a good story is memorable and easy to repeat."

"Right."

"So: clear, concise. What's the third C?"

"Compelling. You need to make sure your stories use words that describe the emotions the people are feeling. What are their struggles? The more you describe someone's problem with empathy, the more they think you have their solution."

"Clear, concise, compelling," Ben repeats.

"Yep," Diane confirms. "Remember I told you I worked for an architecture firm before coming to Athena? That firm built hospitals, and we had to pitch ourselves to get the bid. One time, a colleague told me that when they went to pitch, the hospital said it was going to hire only the people they like the most because they had to work with these people for four years. So my colleague converted his team slide into personal stories with reasons why each person on the team became an architect and where they worked before to increase their likability factor. For example, one person said that he became an architect because he enjoyed playing Legos when he was younger, and now his son plays with Legos, and he joins him because he still has the same passion for the industry as he did as a kid.”

“That’s a really cool story,” Ben says.

“Exactly!” Diane says. “It’s something you’ll remember, right?”

“Totally.”

“Then *they’ll* remember it. And that’s the most important thing. And here I am, repeating it, years later. Another person’s story was that she was in the Israeli army when she was younger, and that’s where she learned all about focus and discipline. She said that her job was to make sure that the project came in under budget, so the army training was perfect. The client loved it! Once the team sells themselves by telling their story of origin, the buyer trusts and likes them and is ready for a case story that will answer the unspoken question: *Will this work for us?* The case story answers this because they see themselves in the story.”

“I can see why. The old way was just telling case studies and showing pictures of a before and after. Or giving details and facts with no story. But if I can turn the before and after into a case *story* that is clear, concise, and compelling, I will win the sale.”

“See? You’re getting it,” Diane says, as she takes the last sip of her coffee.

“It’s hard to unlearn everything I was taught, though,” Ben says and shakes his head. “I learned that people buy logically when they have enough information, which is why I like to constantly push out data and numbers to potential buyers. I really thought there was some magic tipping point, and with just one more fact, people see the light and buy.”

"You need to reframe that thinking. In reality, people buy *emotionally* and then back it up with logic. The best way to tug at people's heartstrings so they open their purse strings is through storytelling. Time and again, when I convert my case studies to case stories, people are intrigued and want to know more. When you turn a boring case study into a compelling case story, you win the sale. For example," Diane goes on, "what did you say to Dell Senton about the Lightning Scalpel?"

"Well, I told them that the Scalpel makes the surgery go 30 percent faster. And who wouldn't want that? I felt like it was a no-brainer."

"Okay," Diane says. "What if you turned those statistics into a story like this: *Imagine how happy Dr. Higgins was at Long Beach Memorial 6 months ago using our equipment when he was able to go out to the patient's family in the waiting room an hour earlier than expected. If you have ever waited for someone you love to come out of surgery, you know every minute feels like an hour. Dr. Higgins put that family out of their waiting misery and said: 'Good news! The scope shows they don't have cancer. They will be fine!' Dr. Higgins said to the rep, 'That's why I became a doctor ... to have moments like that.'* If you tell that story to another doctor at another hospital, they will see themselves in the story and remember why they became a doctor, too. Then they will want that feeling, which makes buying our Lightning Scalpel irresistible."

Silence. "Wow," Ben says after a while. "Now *I* want to buy a Lightning Scalpel!"

They both laugh.

"I'm serious, though," says Ben. "That was amazing. You can really pull people in with a story like that. Not only am I not telling stories, but it also never occurred to me to make the patient's family a character in a story. I see how this makes the doctor the hero in the story."

"Want another one?" Diane asks.

"Yes! Keep them coming. I'll take all the help I can get."

"Okay. Back to my architecture firm. Another time, we won a project because my friend Susan told this story: *Two years ago, City of Hope hired my firm to renovate the hospital waiting area. One of the challenges we faced was creating a place with plenty of light that would help anxious family members relax while waiting for loved ones to come out of surgery, without making it feel like an airport or hotel lounge. And we had to rip up the floors in the middle of the night between 9 p.m. and 6 a.m. to rewire everything.*

We had vendors on call in case something went wrong. Sure enough, at 2 a.m. a fuse blew. We had the vendor there in 20 minutes to fix it. At 5:55 a.m., the last tile went down, and the waiting room was able to open on time. A year later, patient satisfaction scores went up as family members weighed in on the redesign, and we won a Spirit of Life award. Now, we are working on their medical office space."

"What a great story!" Ben says.

"A really great one," Diane agrees. "They then told that story to other hospitals who saw themselves in the story. All they had to say after the story was, *Does that sound like the kind of journey you'd like to go on with us?* Most people would say *Yes!* and they did not even feel pushed into that 'yes.' Storytelling makes closing sales as easy as landing a plane on a clear day."

Ben looks confused. "Landing a plane?"

"Yep! Just start thinking of yourself as a co-pilot with your buyer. You both agree on where you are going before you take off and fly together, even if there is unexpected turbulence. You have a flight plan that you both create and execute together. When I flew back from New York, the pilot came on and said that we were about to land in Austin. Not one person stood up and said, *What?! I thought we were going to fly around forever!*"

Ben laughs into his coffee, and Diane continues, "Yet I hear so many reps and potential clients keep circling around the same topics over and over again. I want to sometimes shout, *Land the plane already!* Nobody has unlimited fuel on a flight or on a sales call. It is really up to the salesperson to set the parameters at the beginning. Sales are lost at the beginning of the process, not the end."

"What do you mean? I have been taught so many different ways to ask for the order, but they still always feel forced and awkward."

Diane nods in recognition. "Start the meeting by getting a 'buy-in' up front. Lead the discussion with the problems, the urgency, and what is at stake. Then talk about the budget upfront and about the ROI now and in the future, and agree on those and talk about who has the most to gain -- and it can't be you!" Diane laughs at this last part, and Ben smiles at her. "Paint the picture. If you don't do this, it is like trying to put together a huge puzzle without seeing the cover of the box. Each sale needs its own blueprint or flight plan."

"Got it," Ben says.

"Then, you can focus on telling stories to pull them along the journey and land the plane, almost on autopilot."

"Now I just need to figure out how to tell a story," Ben says with a laugh.

"We all tell stories all the time! Think about your favorite movie. All good stories have four elements: the exposition, the problem, the solution, and the resolution."

"Okay… I'm listening."

"The *exposition* is where you paint the picture of who, what, and where. The *problem* is when you describe a problem someone else faced so the client sees themselves in your story. The *solution* is where you tell a story that shows you overcoming an obstacle and going the extra mile for a client. And the *resolution* answers questions like what is life like after buying the product?"

"Exposition, problem, solution, resolution. I remember learning that in English class, actually, when I was in college."

"Yep! It's the same thing… a good story, or movie, has all four of those."

"Thanks a lot, Diane. I know you took time out of your weekend to help me. I really appreciate it."

"Not a problem. I'm always happy to help. You'll get there."

Ben smiles and eats the last bite of scone.

Diane stands up and says, "But I really do have to go now. I'm meeting a friend later and have to get ready. Have fun with Clara tonight."

"Thanks! Have fun with your friend. See you Monday."

"Yep, I'll bring the coffee."

Diane heads down the street towards her car, while Ben walks the other way, thinking about everything Diane just said. He knows that the stories Diane told him will stick with him, so it makes sense that they would also stick with the executives he's pitching to. Suddenly, he starts to feel more excited than scared of his next meeting with Dell Senton.

Part 6

By 8 p.m., Ben is exhausted. Barbara said Clara had to be in bed no later than 7:30, but they are on their sixth game of "Go, Fish!" and Clara doesn't even seem remotely tired.

After she wins for the fifth time in a row, Ben says *again* that it's bedtime. She puts up a fight, asking for another round, but Ben knows she's already up too late, and he doesn't want to face Barbara later.

"Fiiiiine," Clara whines.

"Go brush your teeth. I'll meet you in your bedroom," Ben says, laughing to himself about how "adult" that sounds.

By the time Ben walks into Clara's room, she's cuddled under the blanket, waiting. He sits on the edge of her bed, ready for a quick 'goodnight,' but Clara has other ideas.

"Tell me a story?" she asks, with those big brown eyes peering up at him.

How can I say no to that? Ben thinks.

"Uhh, sure," he says, looking around the room for a book. He picks up *Goodnight Moon*, sitting on her bedside table, and opens the cover when Clara says, "Nooooo. That book is boring. Make up a story!"

Ben is about to protest, but the word "story" reminds him of his conversation with Diane that morning. Exposition, problem, solution, resolution, right? He decides his five-year-old niece is the perfect audience for his first attempt at storytelling.

"Okay," Ben says. "Snuggle down."

Clara gets cozy, and Ben reminds himself of the four steps that Diane taught him earlier: exposition, problem, solution, resolution.

He starts a story "Once upon a time there was a little girl who wanted to be a knight when she grew up. She was five years old just like you, and her name was Lauren."

Ben goes on to describe the challenges little Lauren faced as she grew up. Most people said little girls could never grow up to be knights, but Lauren learned to never give up trying.

By the end of the story, Lauren, not so little anymore, wins her first tournament and rides off into the sunset, excited for the next one.

When he finishes, Ben looks at Clara, and she is smiling ear-to-ear.

"That was *such* a great story! I want to be a knight, too!" Clara beams.

Ben laughs and gives her a quick kiss on the forehead. "Goodnight, Clara. For real. Bedtime."

Ben retires to the kitchen table, feeling pretty good about his storytelling. He included the exposition, the problem, the solution, and the resolution, and it felt complete. Clara definitely liked it, at least.

He spends the rest of the night on his computer, thinking about storytelling and his own story of origin. Diane really impressed him with the stories of origin that the architects told to win the project, and he would absolutely remember them. He wants to make sure his own origin story is just as memorable.

Ben wakes up groggy the next morning. Barbara and Dave got home later than they expected, and Ben didn't crawl into his own bed until one o'clock in the morning. But he told Jason he'd meet him for a run this morning, so he takes a quick shower to wake up before throwing on his clothes and sneakers and heading out the door.

"Hey, Jason," Ben greets his friend as he gets out of the car. Jason is parked two spots over and is stretching his hamstrings like a "real" runner.

"Hey, Buddy!" Jason calls out.

Ben walks over to Jason and starts mimicking his stretches.

"Ready to hit the pavement?" Jason finally asks.

Ben nods, and he follows Jason to the path. Once there, they start with a comfortable, soft jog. Nothing too strenuous, for which Ben is thankful.

They fall into familiar conversation, filling each other in on their weekends. Ben tells Jason about babysitting last night and how exhausting a five-year-old can be, and then he mentions a girl he met on Tinder last month, Audrey. They've gone on a few dates, and Ben tells Jason how things seem to be getting more serious.

In return, Jason tells a very funny, and painful, story about a Tinder-date-gone-wrong that he had last night.

Jason said he was so nervous on the date that he spilled a drink on himself *and* stepped on her foot when they were walking back to the car after dinner. As if that wasn't bad enough, he wound up getting lost driving her home. She was *not* happy when he finally pulled up to her apartment building.

Ben stops jogging at one point because he's laughing so hard. Jason stops, too, smiling despite himself.

"Now *that* was a funny story," Ben says when he recovers.

"Thanks for enjoying my pain," Jason laughs and rolls his eyes.

"No, I'm serious. That was a great story! Did I tell you I met Diane for coffee yesterday morning? She is convinced that I need to tell better stories in my sales meetings. Case stories, she called them."

"Oh?" Jason asks, as he starts to walk.

Ben falls into stride with him. "Yes. She said that pushing out facts and figures just doesn't work anymore. I need to answer the question, *Will this work for me?* and help buyers see themselves in the story. Let them know I have their solution."

"Absolutely, man! I do something similar."

"You do?"

"Yep," Jason replies. "One time, I was selling that monitor – remember the 4K resolution one? That thing is amazing."

Ben nods in recognition. "Yes, it is really great."

"Well, I was trained to push out information about the pixels in the resolution, and the numbers were so impressive! But it's hard to sell pixels to a hospital, you know?

"Sure," Ben agrees.

"Then the tech guy told me a story about a hospital in Minnesota that had tested the monitor. There was a patient who had a very high BMI, which put him at a high risk during surgery. The tech rep was in the room with the doctor during the surgery and because of the high risk, the doctor hit a bleeder. It was a sea of red, and everyone in the operating room took a deep breath and held it, wondering how fast the doctor was going to be able to find the source of the bleeding and save the patient's life."

"Geeez," Ben whispers.

"I know. So then the doctor calmly remembers to look at the resolution monitor, where he could see subtle differences in the colors of red, determining which blood was oxygenated and which was not. That allowed him to instantly pick the fastest and right way to find the source of that bleeder and save the patient's life."

"Wow! That's cool!"

"Totally cool. After the surgery, the doctor turned to the tech guy and said something like 'We don't always need a monitor like that for a surgery, but boy when we need it, we need it.'"

"Excellent resolution," Ben says.

"Huh? In the screen?" Jason asks, confused.

"No, in the story. The resolution. The 'what is life like with this product' question that ends every good case story."

"Oh, I get it. Right, exactly. Like, life would have been pretty different for that patient – and I'd imagine for the doctor, too – without the monitor. So *then*, I told that story at my next sales meeting, and it allowed everyone in the room to imagine themselves in that situation. No one wants to go blindly into guessing where the source of the bleeder is. It's kind of like flying an airplane on a clear, beautiful day. You probably don't need all of the GPS information because you can trust your eyes. But if a sudden storm hits, you might be confused as to what's up or what's down, and you'll be glad you have state-of-the-art technology in your plane. Same thing goes for a doctor in the operating room."

Ben thinks about this as they fall back into a slow jog. That story was so memorable, and it was also clear, concise, and compelling. Who wouldn't want to buy that monitor after knowing how quickly it saved someone's life? That's not something that pixel numbers could ever accurately convey.

He's not sure what his next step is, but it's obvious to Ben that he needs to start focusing on how to tell case stories that compel people and draw them in.

The next day, Ben finds Diane sitting in his cubicle, sipping her coffee and scrolling through her phone. His own coffee, correctly labeled "Ben," was sitting next to his keyboard.

"Morning, Diane," Ben says.

"Morning!" Diane answers brightly. She gets up from Ben's chair and points to his coffee. "For you."

"Thanks," Ben replies. "What's on the agenda today?"

Diane checks her calendar on her phone. "I'm meeting with Julie about the new product I've been working on, RadarPulse."

"That sounds really powerful." Ben drops his backpack to the floor and sinks into his chair.

"It is. And ready to be sold."

"Awesome. Maybe I can convince Julie to give me a sneak peek."

"I'll put in a good word," Diane says. "What's your day looking like?"

Ben bends down to turn on his computer before answering. "Preparation. I will meet with Dr. Palin at DHR next week, and after talking to you and Jason this weekend, I'm ready to take my storytelling skills to the next level."

"Great! Well, let me know if you need anything. I'll see you later."

"Will do, thanks. Bye, Diane."

"See ya!"

By midafternoon, Ben is exhausted. He spent the day researching DHR hospital and recalling everything Diane told him about the Lightning Scalpel as he attempted to write stories. He wrote "clear, concise, and compelling" on a Post-it and stuck it to his computer, which was a good reminder to him as he tried to write memorable and magnetic stories.

A Slack message pops up in the sales rep channel from Julie:

Hello, @here! Now that I'm settled in my new position, I'd like to begin weekly meetings every Wednesday afternoon. Y'all will have the invite shortly. These will be informal check-ins, and if there is ever anything you'd like to share or discuss, please bring it to my attention. Thanks! Looking forward to our first meeting on Wednesday.

Ben sighs to himself, careful to not let anyone around him hear. The office around him becomes eerily quiet as, he assumes, everyone is reading the message and wondering what these "informal check-ins" really mean.

Julie is really leaning into the new job, Ben thinks.

On Wednesday, Ben files into the conference room at two o'clock and grabs a seat next to Jason.

"Hey, Buddy," Jason says as Ben opens a fresh Google Doc on his MacBook. "Taking notes?"

"I'm going to at least look like it," Ben replies, looking accusingly at the empty table in front of Jason.

Jason looks at the table and then back at Ben, and then quickly takes his laptop out of the backpack at his feet.

Julie walks in at that moment, beaming down at the eight reps sitting around the conference table.

"Hi!" she says, a bit too enthusiastically.

Everyone greets her back kindly, and Julie takes a seat at the head of the table, which was unilaterally kept open for her. She opens a notebook to a page with some writing and pulls a pen out from behind her ear.

"Okay, then," she begins. "Thank you all for accepting the weekly invitation. I know this isn't typically something that Carl would do," she says with a knowing smile, "but I think that we all want the same thing – to win more sales – and I know the way to do this is by raising team morale, sharing our wins and our stories, and learning from everyone's mistakes. We shouldn't work in a vacuum, in other words."

Ben nods. That all makes sense to him, and he would love to hear other people's stories so that he can incorporate them into his own toolbox.

"So. I'd like to start each meeting with our wins. And this doesn't have to be a professional win, either. I believe that acts of kindness are the best way to gather those wins. I even keep a note on my white board in my office, which some of you have already seen. It says ABK."

At this, Julie stands up and grabs a black dry-erase marker. She writes ABK on the white board behind her.

She turns around, looking down at everyone around the table. "Always. Be. Kind. My play on ABC: Always Be Closing. Closing is great, for sure, but I really don't think we can ever get there without kindness. I want you to all remember this in your client meetings. Kindness goes a long way. In fact, I'd like to start out these meetings each week with an example of your kindness, either professionally or personally. We can consider these our 'wins' for the week, as we work towards fulfilling Athena's company goals: charity, loyalty, flexibility. We don't want to be ruthless. We want to be kind, right?"

Everyone around the table nods, and Ben writes "ABK" in his notebook, and Jason pokes him in the ribs with his elbow, as if to make fun of him. *Whatever*, Ben thinks. *This is my year.*

"So," Julie continues, as she sits back down, "what is an example of a win you've had recently, either an example of progress or an example of kindness?"

No one speaks. No one even moves, out of fear of being called on.

"I'll go first," she ventures. "It was Shari Gold's birthday last week, the office manager who's been with Dr. Livingston at MD Anderson for 10 years. She really runs that whole office … and his life." At this, everyone in the room laughs knowingly.

Julie goes on. "I've known her for years. I had marked down when her birthday was and coordinated with her team to give her a little surprise birthday. Dr. Livingston was very grateful, especially since there were some years when he forgot. But this birthday, he looked like a hero to Shari. And that's something he'll remember the next time I go to see him for a meeting."

"Wow," says Monica, the sales rep seated to Julie's left. "I would have never thought to do something like that."

"It's small," said Julie, "but we have to remember that everyone we're dealing with here are actual people, too. They have feelings and lives and stories. And people like to be treated like, well, people. You know?"

Everyone nods again, but it's not quite clear that everyone is buying this yet.

Julie is able to pull some forced kindness stories out of a few other unsure reps, and then she steers the meeting in a different direction, going over numbers and projections. In the past, Carl would have *only* focused on those numbers, but Julie's way of starting meetings with "wins" and soft skills seems to Ben like a great way to build morale.

Finally, Julie dismisses everyone and reminds them to bring their "wins" to next week's meeting.

Ben and Jason leave together, and Jason asks while they walk, "What do you think of all that? Being kind, getting involved in people's lives?"

Ben thinks for a moment and then replies, "I think it can't hurt, right? I mean, I hate feeling like 'just another sales rep' when I get into a meeting, so it makes sense that people don't want to be thought of as 'just another doctor' or 'just another executive.'"

"Yes, that's true," Jason says. "I guess I'll try to participate in Julie's little experiment, too."

"Good idea. What's the worst that could happen? You accidentally spread too much kindness?" Ben jokes.

"Very funny," says Jason. "I'll see ya later!"

Jason disappears into the men's room, while Ben continues on to his cubicle, with a newfound determination to create clear, concise, and compelling stories that people can see themselves in.

The next Tuesday, Ben walks into his sales meeting with DHR feeling more ready and confident than ever. He's written at the top of his notecard: "3 Cs" and "ABK," the two abbreviations that have gotten him through this past week.

Ben greets Dr. Palin and the two executives warmly, having just stacked his moments of certainty on his way to the meeting. Once they trade pleasantries, Ben begins pitching the Lightning Scalpel. But instead of launching into those very impressive numbers, Ben uses Diane's story to start his pitch:

"Earlier this year at Long Beach Memorial, Dr. Higgins was using the Lightning Scalpel, which helps surgeries go 30% faster. Imagine how happy Dr. Higgins was at Long Beach Memorial 6 months ago using our equipment when he was able to go out to the patient's family in the waiting room an hour earlier than expected. If you have ever waited for someone you love to come out of surgery, you know every minute feels like an hour. Dr. Higgins put that family out of their waiting misery and said: 'Good news! The scope shows they don't have cancer. They will be fine!' Dr. Higgins said to the rep, 'That's why I became a doctor ... to have moments like that.'"

Just as Diane promised, Dr. Palin slams his hand on the table and says, "Yes! That's why I become a doctor, too!"

Ben is almost stunned into silence, shocked that the story already worked so well. But he quickly recovers and continues talking about how the Lightning Scalpel can improve the lives of the doctors, patients, and the patients' families. The doctor and executives all nod along, looking truly interested and impressed.

And yes, Ben even plays his video, stored locally on his computer's hard drive.

By the time Ben leaves the meeting, he feels a camaraderie with the people in the room, and he is confident and happy with himself.

He sits in his car in the parking lot and texts Diane to tell her that her story really worked.

Even if I don't get the sale, Ben writes, *I can feel myself getting closer. I feel like I'm already improving. I felt better in there than I have in any recent sales calls.*

Diane texts back a quick *Yay!! Can't wait to hear more.*

Ben puts his phone down and drives back to the office with a smile on his face.

The next day is the second team meeting with Julie. When Ben gets to the conference room, he sees that Jason's computer is already open, and when Ben sits down next to him, he makes a show of looking at the computer and then back at Jason in disbelief.

"C'mon, man," Jason says, laughing. "I said I'd try!"

"Okay, okay," Ben answers, putting his hands up in surrender.

Julie walks in and takes her now-assigned seat at the head of the table.

"Hi, everyone!" she greets the reps. "What a week, right? Only Wednesday, and it feels like I've done a week's worth of work already."

Everyone laughs in agreement, and Julie gets down to business.

"So, does everyone have their wins ready this week, now that you had a week to prepare?" She looks around the room. "Yes? Good. Does someone else want to start this week?

The first person to go, a first-year rep named Peter, tells a story about how he spent his weekend volunteering at his alma mater, giving campus tours and doing interviews.

Grace talks about getting a second meeting with Franklin Medical Center, and Theo says that he won a sale he was working on for a long time. At that, the table erupts into applause, and Ben has to hand it to Julie. It really is nice celebrating wins with a group of people.

Monica goes next. She says, "I asked Dr. Chin at Austin Health Hospital to give us a testimonial about how our products have been helping them save time and money, and she said yes!"

"That is wonderful," Julie says. "And actually, it's the perfect segue into the next order of business for today. I talked to Carl, and we hired someone to create a repository map of all new testimonials and some of the previous case stories."

"Case stories?" Ben asks aloud, before he can stop himself.

"Yes! Diane and I had such a great meeting last week about a new product, and she introduced me to the idea of case stories, and I thought it just made so much sense. It gave a name to something that I realized I was already doing the whole time! Who knew?!"

As Julie launches into a description of case stories for everyone in the conference room, Ben finds his mind wandering.

How does everyone know this? he wonders. *No wonder I wasn't winning any sales. The one with the story is the one who wins the sale. The sale is literally in the tale!*

Ben comes back to earth as he hears his name. "Ben?" Julie is saying. "Diane said that you have already been working with her on your case stories."

"Yep," Ben says. "Actually, I used one of her stories in my pitch meeting yesterday, and it went really, really well."

"Great!" Julie says. "That's your win for the week?"

"Not quite. I was going to say that my win for the week came after that. I thought about what you said about being kind, so when I got back to my desk, I emailed Diane and copied her boss Uma, just to thank her for helping me and letting her know how great it went."

"Really nice, Ben. What a good idea to copy Uma, too," Julie says approvingly.

"Thanks. Uma wrote back, too, that she agrees Diane is one of the best."

"Wonderful! Wins all around. And that's ABK in action. Anytime you can acknowledge someone's contribution, whether they're a coworker in another division or a client, it is a win."

Julie moves on to explain some more about the repository. Her plan is to have everyone submit case stories, and then someone can compile them into a central location. Then, everyone on the team will have access to them. She calls it a "playlist" of case stories, which team members can pick and choose from, based on the type of client they are working with.

"Think about it," Julie says. "Everyone has different personalities and responds to things differently, right? There are various *avatars* of clients, and if we have a central repository of case stories, you can each choose a story that best fits that avatar. Maybe your client responds better to facts? Maybe he or she responds to an emotional story? Whatever type of avatar you are pitching to, you will have a playlist of stories queued up and ready to go."

Ben likes the sound of that. He has a few case stories that he thought of throughout the week, and Diane shared hers, too. But if there was a central location where everyone could share their case stories, he would have a ton to choose from.

While Ben is considering this, Julie asks the group, "Does anyone ever feel like they're stuck in the friend zone at work?"

By looking around the table, Ben can tell that everyone is as confused as he is.

"Can you explain what you mean by that?" Monica asks the question that no one else dared to.

"Of course," Julie answers. "We all get so excited when a potential client says *I'm interested! Send me some info.* In our heads, we think it's at least 50/50 that they will buy from us. But the reality is less than ten percent of those sales actually happen. And why? Because we are stuck in the friend zone at work. Instead of giving us a *no*, they placate us with *I'm interested* or *let me think about it* or *I need more information.* But remember: people buy *emotionally* not logically. We never lose a sale because the client doesn't have enough information. We lose it because we have not told a story that is compelling enough to make them fix their problem. We need to work on stories where potential clients can see themselves in the story."

This makes sense to Ben. Listening to Julie explain it, he realizes that he's often felt as if he's stuck in the friend zone at work. He is good at what he does, but he can't seem to push through the friend zone to get to the point when the clients are intrigued and find what he's saying to be irresistible.

How do I go from invisible to irresistible? he wonders. *How do I get out of this "friend zone"?*

Ben knew all too well what it felt like to be in the friend zone in his dating life. The love of his life in college was a girl named Mary who was fun and the life of the party. While they always had a good time together, she said she just didn't see them as any more than friends.

His friend Charlie had said, *Once you're in the friend zone with a girl you can never get out of it*. Then one night when he was saying goodbye, Mary told him that it felt like kissing her brother. That one really hurt.

Ben is determined to not get stuck at the friend zone at work and let another big sale or promotion pass him by.

"Okay," Julie says. "Next week, I'd like each of you to come in with a client with whom you feel you're stuck in the friend zone at work. Then as a group, we will brainstorm what story to tell them that intrigues them enough to re-engage with us. As a group, we will share our previous stories of what has worked so we can have the right story to go. Anything else for this week? Anyone?"

No one says anything, so Julie dismisses them, and Ben and Jason walk out together again.

"Great job in there," Jason says.

"Thanks."

"I really need to work on my win for next week," he groans.

"Let me know if you want help!" Ben calls, as he turns left towards his cubicle.

On Friday afternoon, Julie Slacks Ben.

Hey @Ben. Do you have a minute?

Sure, Ben writes back. *See you soon.*

Previously, a message like that would have scared Ben straight, but Ben feels so confident in his improvement lately that he doesn't dread walking into Julie's office.

"Hi, Julie," he says while rapping lighting on her opened office door.

"Hey, Ben! Come on in."

"Door open or closed?"

"Depends how loudly you're going to cheer when I tell you that you won the DHR pitch from earlier in the week!" she says excitedly.

"So, closed!" Ben practically yells while shutting the door behind him, laughing. "Wow, that's just great, Julie. I felt it, too. I felt myself making that sale."

"I can tell. You were like a different person in our meeting on Wednesday. You seemed so calm and happy."

"I *am* calm and happy! Well, happier now. This is great news."

"It is great news. And the even better news is that not only did they accept, but they also spoke very highly of you in their email to me. And, taking a cue from your book, I copied Carl on my response to them, so he also saw what a great sales rep you are."

Ben falls back into the chair across from where Julie is sitting at her desk.

"Wow, Julie. That's so kind of you. Thank you."

"ABK!" they both exclaim in unison, laughing.

"Seriously, though," Ben says. "Thank you for recognizing my hard work."

"You're very welcome," Julie responds. "Keep it up. We have plenty of work ahead of us."

"Yes ma'am," Ben answers.

They talk a bit more about implementing case stories and the new repository map that is being compiled before Ben thanks Julie again and stands up.

"I can't wait to see what you do next," Julie says.

"Neither can I!" Ben answers on his way out the door.

Part 7

For the first time in a long time, Ben is excited to get to work on Monday morning. He's already sitting at his desk when Diane shows up with Monday morning coffees.

"Hey, Ben!" Diane exclaims, surprised to see him there already. "I'm usually the first one here!"

Ben turns around in his chair and smiles. "I know. I just felt so good after talking to Julie on Friday afternoon, I was excited to get back into the swing of things."

He couldn't stop thinking about that all weekend. When he met Barbara for their bike ride on Saturday, Ben told Barbara about the pitch meeting, and she cheered with him when he ended his story with the meeting with Julie on Friday afternoon.

He even called his mom yesterday and shared the news with her and his dad. He hadn't told them about losing the promotion yet, but he decided yesterday was as good a time as any to catch them up on things, especially since he had good news to give them at the end.

They were understanding, of course, and they encouraged him to "keep up the good work!" and "go get 'em!" and all those things that parents say when they don't know what else to say.

"I know," Diane says. "I was thinking about your big win this weekend, too. I'm so happy that you are getting the hang of the case stories and that it's working for you."

"Me, too. I really appreciate you helping me out."

"You're very welcome," Diane says before turning around and heading to her cubicle.

Ben sits down at his desk and turns his computer on. Once it powers up and he opens his mail, he finds a calendar invite from Julie for today at 11. She labeled it "Repository Brainstorm."

Interesting, Ben thinks, as he clicks 'Accept.'

When he gets to Julie's office at 11, he finds the door open, and Julie is sitting in one of the two chairs across from her desk.

"Hi, Julie," Ben says as he walks in. He shuts the door behind him and takes a seat next to Julie.

"Hey, Ben! Thanks so much for coming by. I have something I'd like to run by you."

"Of course, I'd love to hear it."

"In our weekly meeting last week, I mentioned creating a repository map of case stories that our sales reps can use in pitch meetings."

"Yes," Ben replies. "I think it's such a great idea. That way, we don't need to keep creating stories of our own. We can work as a team and use each other for our case stories. I did it myself at the meeting last week. I used Diane's story, and it obviously worked."

"Exactly. Which is why I wanted to talk to you. Do you have any interest in spearheading this repository? You'd be responsible for compiling and keeping track of the stories. I have someone in IT who can deal with the technical logistics of creating a virtual repository, but we need a point person to talk to the sales reps and make sure everyone has something to contribute."

Ben grins widely. "I would love to do that, Julie."

"Really?" she asks. "It wouldn't be too much extra work, but I think it would be really good for you. And for Carl."

"Carl?"

"Well, I'm trying to convince him of how important stories are, and him seeing them all in one place could be a great start. Also, I think it'll help your case if Carl knows that you are stepping up in this way."

Ben thinks for a moment, and nods. "True. I've been trying to figure out a way that I can contribute to the company in a meaningful way, and I really think this is the answer. Thanks a lot for the opportunity, Julie."

"You got it," Julie says. "So at our meeting on Wednesday, I'll announce you as the case story repository point person, good?"

"Good."

Julie stands up, and Ben does the same.

"Thanks again," he says one last time as he moves towards the door. "This is going to be fun."

Julie smiles and sits down behind her desk with a wave as Ben leaves.

On Wednesday, Ben walks into the office and actually finds himself excited for the weekly meeting this afternoon. For one thing, he absolutely has his win since DHR said yes! Plus, he is the new point person for the repository map, which will arm him with more and more stories to keep winning sales.

But he has work to do before the meeting, and today, Ben feels ready and confident to take on his pitch meeting next week, with Methodist Hospital in San Antonio.

Julie opens that afternoon meeting by asking for people's wins for the week, as usual. Theo made a sale last week, too, so he and Ben talked about how the pitch meetings went, and what they think sealed the deal. They shared the case stories that they used, and Ben was careful to type down Theo's story to use for the repository.

Once everyone shared, Julie again talked about sales numbers, which look good, and projections, which are promising. She then says, "And I wanted to circle back to the case story repository map. I've asked Ben to lead that project, so you can expect an email from him about what he needs from each of you. Anything else, Ben?"

Julie looks up at Ben expectantly. Ben wasn't expecting to be addressing the team like this, at least not today.

He clears his throat. "Umm, yes. No. I mean, thanks, Julie. I'm happy to do this." He forces himself to look away from Julie and at his co-workers, who are all staring at him, looking like he should say more.

Ben goes on. "Like Julie said, I'll email you all shortly. I know Julie went over case stories last week, but I'm happy to answer any questions you might have during these meetings or anytime through Slack or email. I'm here." He laughs a bit nervously and looks down at his hands.

Julie takes over from there. "So, great! Thanks again, Ben. And I'll see you all in the hallways, right? My door is always open."

Ben and Jason leave together again, and Jason claps a hand on Ben's back.

"Nice, man!" he says.

"Yeah?" Ben replies questioningly.

"For sure. It's good to see you getting involved in the company more and taking on a leadership role."

"Thanks," Ben replies. "It feels good, too."

The men smile at each other before going their separate ways at the end of the hall.

The next day, Ben sends an email to the eight sales reps, asking them for their case stories.

What is a case story? he writes. *Remember that it is a story that allows the buyer to see themselves as the hero. The story should be clear, concise, and compelling and include four parts: the exposition, the problem, the solution, and the resolution.*

He goes on to explain how to properly submit their case stories via Google Drive, and he makes sure to remind them to reach out to him with any questions.

Just before he clicks "Send" he BCC's Diane, so she can see first-hand how far he's come because of her.

Ten minutes later, Diane materializes behind Ben.

"Ben! I didn't know that this was your project!" she exclaims.

Ben turns around in his chair and smiles up at her. "It wasn't, until Julie gave it to me earlier this week. Isn't that great? And it's all thanks to you!"

"No way. You did all the leg work. Great job, I'm so happy for you."

"Thanks!" Ben replies.

"What are you doing tomorrow night? Want to meet at Otopia for celebratory drinks? On you, of course."

Ben laughs. "Sure. 7?"

"See you there!" Diane calls as she turns and walks away.

At 7 p.m. the next night, Ben walks into the crowded bar, not sure if they'll be able to grab a seat. But then he spots Diane already there, with her handbag on the bar stool next to her.

"Hey!" she calls when she sees Ben, grabbing her bag and pointing to the stool.

"Hey, back," Ben says, taking a seat. "Good call getting here early."

"I figured it would get busy. Anyway, I ordered you a glass of wine," Diane says just as the bartender places a glass of white in front of Ben.

Diane raises her own glass in a toast: "To you!"

"And to you," Ben replies, as they clink glasses and take a sip.

After they place their glasses down, Ben says, "But really. I couldn't have done this without you."

"That's what friends are for. Plus, the number one rule is don't go it alone! A healthy ego is one that realizes it can't do everything alone and needs other people to help."

"It's true," Ben says thoughtfully. "If you think you can do everything by yourself, you won't get very far."

"Yep. There's an African proverb that says, 'If you want to go fast, go alone; but if you want to go far, go together.'"

"I like that. Go together."

"Remember when I broke my leg over the summer? My mom had to move in with me for two weeks! I was helpless."

"I do remember that." Ben nods in recognition.

"When I was growing up, I was taught that asking for help was a form of weakness. It took decades for me to realize how wrong that is. Sometimes, trying to do everything yourself causes you to never get anything done. I even think that letting other people help you in your career and in your personal life is a form of self-love. You love yourself enough to let others give you what you need"

"All good points. And actually, that's what we're doing with the repository map," Ben says. "Don't go it alone. We are relying on each other for stories and help, rather than working in a vacuum."

Diane nods as she takes a sip. "That's so true, Ben. That's definitely an example of 'going together.'"

"I really think it's going to help everyone, myself included. I'm excited to see it all come together. Julie said that she's trying to get Carl on board with the whole storytelling idea, and she thinks this will be a big step towards that. Hopefully I can make them both happy."

"I'm sure you will," says Diane.

"Okay. Now that we got that out of the way, can we talk about something that's not work? What's new with you?"

Ben and Diane spend the rest of the evening talking about anything but work, and Ben heads home feeling happy and confident. He doesn't even mind when his Uber driver takes him the long way home.

On Monday morning, Ben is sitting at his desk when Diane knocks on his cubicle awkwardly, hands full of coffee.

"Hey, Diane," Ben says before even swiveling his chair around. He could smell the coffee from down the hall.

"Morning, Ben." Diane hands his coffee over and leans against the entrance of the cubicle. "How was the rest of your weekend?"

"Really good. I kept checking Google Drive to see if anyone had uploaded their case stories."

"And?"

"Nothing yet."

Diane gave a sympathetic laugh. "That's the problem with being a manager, I guess. No one listens!"

Ben smiles. "I guess I still have a lot to learn. But the other thing I did this weekend was go over our conversation at Mozart's before I went to babysit Clara the other week. You talked about something else before case stories. You mentioned people's origins?"

Diane nods. "Yes, their stories of origin."

"Right. And I remember those stories – about playing with Legos, the Israeli army. So I was thinking: in addition to product case stories, why don't I ask everyone for their story of origin, too?"

"I like that idea a lot," Diane replies. "Run it by Julie? See what she thinks?"

"Already composing an email!" Ben points to his screen, which has an open, blank email. "Well, almost."

Diane laughs and stands up straight. "Okay, work time. Talk to you later."

They both wave, and Diane heads towards her cubicle on the other side of the office.

Ben spends the better part of the hour drafting an email to Julie, explaining what he has learned about stories of origin and asking if he should ask the reps to include theirs as well.

Julie writes back later that afternoon: *Interesting thought. I haven't considered stories of origin much. Before I sign off on this idea, tell me: What is your story of origin?*

Not quite the answer Ben was expecting. He was so busy congratulating himself for a great idea that he didn't even consider his own story of origin.

Of course I would need to include my own, he thinks. He looks at the clock: 4:25. Ben decides it's just late enough into the day that he can get away with answering Julie tomorrow morning. Tonight, he has his work cut out for him, trying to figure out how he got to where he is now.

The next morning, Ben gets to his cubicle at 7:55 a.m. and turns his computer on. Once powered up, Ben heads to Google Drive to recover what he wrote last night. He worked on his story of origin for hours. If Julie had asked Ben even last week how he got into medical supply sales, he would have probably made a joke about how he does it "for the money."

But now that he knows how important stories of origin are, he really takes the time to consider *How did I get here?*

It took some digging and soul-searching, but Ben was finally able to write out his story of origin. And it surprised even himself.

He copies and pastes it into a reply email to Julie, and reads it over once more before hitting send:

I became a medical sales representative almost by accident. When I began college at the University of Illinois, I was an undeclared major. I had no idea what I wanted to do. The only thing I knew for sure was that I was obsessed with gaming and messing around with computers. I was always researching and waiting for the next best thing to come out for me to tinker with. But by the end of freshman year, my father convinced me to major in business, since that would open many different doors.

So I began sophomore year working towards my B.S. in Business. And then my mother was diagnosed with breast cancer. It shook our small, suburban, insulated world, and my father was so upset that he often needed taking care of, too. My sister, Barbara, and I really had to step up and help my family.

My mom had a double mastectomy and then underwent both chemo and radiation, and I really had a front-row seat to all that she went through. It was a lot of medicine and medical devices and doctors and medical jargon. And I knew my mother was suffering, but she was also getting better. And I really felt drawn to that world. The medical world. The world of 'making people feel better.'

When it was time to choose an internship, I only applied to medical supply companies because they combined two of my favorite things: emerging technologies and the medical industry. And I get to help people feel better while I do it. What could be better?

Ben must admit: He wasn't even sure where that came from. He did grow up loving game systems and computers, and he was really fascinated by all of the medical devices surrounding his mom. But he never really made that connection before.

He hits "Send," and his email is off to the cloud, landing in Julie's inbox right about now.

Nothing to do but wait. In the meantime, Ben continues his preparation for the Methodist Hospital pitch on Thursday. He plans on using the same case story that he told DHL two weeks ago because, well, it worked. But he spends time researching the hospital and the doctor, Dr. Domingo, whom he'll be meeting with.

Two days later, Ben still hasn't heard back from Julie about his story of origin. He walks into the weekly meeting feeling a bit rejected, especially after he put so much work into his story. He even sent it to Diane to read, and Diane said it brought her to tears! But Ben knows that Julie was out yesterday, so he assumes she just got busy.

After everyone is in the conference room, Julie rushes in and takes her seat.

"Hi, all!"

"Hi, Julie," everyone responds in unison, as if they were in a first-grade classroom.

They start the meeting as usual, with their wins. Patrick sent 'thank you' cookies to the front office of the hospital he met with last week. Monica convinced one of her hospitals to extend their contract. Grace adopted a dog.

Once everyone is done sharing, Julie turns to Ben. "Did you send out your email yet? I didn't see it. Was I not copied on it?"

Ben looks up at her and then looks around, trying to figure out what she is talking about.

"I'm sorry, what email are you referring to?" Ben asks.

"The story of origin email! I thought you were going to share yours and ask everyone to share theirs."

"Oh. I didn't hear back from you, so I wasn't sure…"

"But I responded right away!" Julie exclaims. I so enjoyed reading your story of origin, and I really can't wait to read the rest of them."

"You did? I didn't see an email!" Ben says, as he opens his work email on his phone. Scrolling through, he shakes his head as he doesn't see anything. "No, nothing."

"Weird! Let me check," Julie says, as she starts scrolling through her own phone. "Oh no! It didn't send! It looks like it's still sitting in my drafts. I'm so sorry about that, Ben. Let me send it right now."

She clicks a button and then puts her phone down.

"What I said, though, was that I really loved reading your story. I learned so much about you, and I appreciate you sharing it. I think it's a great idea for everyone to share theirs as we build the repository."

Ben puts his phone down, too, and flushes slightly. "Well, that's great, Julie. Thanks a lot. I had a lot of fun writing it, so I'm glad you liked it."

Jason kicks Ben under the table in a way that clearly means "Teacher's Pet," but Ben doesn't mind. He's just happy to be on the right track again.

Julie doesn't see any of this and continues. "I really look forward to getting to better know you all. Then we can practice telling our case stories and stories of origin with each other. That way, when you have a request to pitch for new business, you are ready to go! It's also a great thing to ask a new client. You can ask how they got into the business. It makes for great conversations around meals, too. Asking people for their own stories of origin gets them to open up."

Julie asks Ben to explain more about what a story of origin is, and Ben addresses the table, explaining that the story of origin is meant to explain the *How I got here* question and act to connect to the person you're talking to.

When Monica asks to hear Ben's story, Ben circumvents her request: "I'll email it to you all," he says instead. "And please do remember to send in your case stories, too. The quicker we get this map up and running, the more connections – and money! – we can all make."

Everyone lets out a small cheer, and Julie moves on to other business.

Jason teases Ben a bit on their way out of the meeting, but Ben is too excited about his future to even care at this point. He feels himself becoming a better salesperson and employee – and person.

For the next month, Ben keeps his head down and really hones his storytelling skills as he compiles the case stories for the repository. Using the Lightning Scalpel story and his story of origin, along with his tried-and-true professional sales skills, Ben easily wins the Methodist Hospital bid (turns out, when Ben was telling his story of origin, Dr. Domingo liked playing with computers as a teenager, too!).

Since then, he had made two other big sales and one smaller one, and Julie seems pleased with his progress.

And one time, he walked by Carl in the hallway, and – get ready for this – Carl just nodded and kept walking! Ben couldn't believe his good luck.

But all of that means very little because next Wednesday, on December 1, Ben has his second meeting with Dell Senton. This wouldn't necessarily be a bad thing in its own right, because Ben feels calm and prepared, but he walked in to work today and had this email sitting in his inbox from Kara:

Good morning, Ben!

Wanted to let you know Carl will be attending the Dell Senton meeting with you next week. Lucky you!

He'll meet you there. He said to make sure you're ready for this.

Kara

Ben isn't sure if the "Lucky you!" is sincere or sarcastic, but either way, it's not helpful. Since that email, Ben's spent his day wondering if his storytelling skills are enough to impress Carl, or if Carl would just think he's some hack who can't sell properly.

Julie presented the case story repository to Carl once again, after Frederico in IT mocked up an interactive map with some of the stories loaded in. Ben wasn't a part of that meeting, but Julie reported that Carl seemed "not entirely *un*interested," so Ben assumed that was a good thing.

But no matter how many sales Ben has made since the MD Anderson pitch meeting where he bombed in front of Carl, he can't shake the feeling of a kid being sent to detention for doing something wrong. This was going to throw a wrench in things.

As Ben pulls into the Dell Senton parking lot on the day of the meeting, he feels the familiar feeling of dread. He desperately tries to remember his moments of certainty, but he keeps drawing blanks, and the only moment he can seem to remember is the moment he realized the video wasn't playing in that stuffy closet-of-a-conference room. His heart starts racing, and he feels sweat forming on the back of his neck.

Ben! Get a hold of yourself! He attempts to give himself a pep talk.

Will this matter in 5 minutes? Well yes, of course!

Will it matter in 5 days? Absolutely, this pitch will matter in 5 days.

5 weeks? 5 months? It might!

5 years? Well… no, of course not. This pitch will not matter in five years.

Ben sits in his car and pictures 5-years-from-now Ben laughing at today-Ben for being so worked up and nervous.

He also notices that 5-years-from-now Ben is *not* living in a basement apartment, so at least that's a good thing.

Okay. Breathe. Ben coaches himself.

When he looks up, he sees a large, commanding-looking man standing at the entrance of the building, staring at his watch. Carl.

It's go-time.

"Hi, Carl!" Ben practically yells as his jogs across the street to him, narrowly dodging a bicyclist while Carl watches on in agitation.

When Ben successfully crosses the street, Carl simply points to his watch and pushes his way through the revolving doors into the building.

Ben has no choice but to follow behind like a sad puppy.

By the time the elevator doors open on the fourth floor, Carl still has not said a word to Ben, other than a few grunts in answer to Ben's questions: "How's your day going?", "Any traffic?", "Dell Senton, am I right?" (Ben doesn't even know what that last question means.)

By two o'clock, they are all sitting around a large oval table in a larger-than-life conference room. It's much too large for the five people who are there, which makes it even more difficult for Ben to imagine making a connection with anyone.

Dr. Ji welcomes Ben and Carl, and then immediately asks if they can be quick because he has to get to an appointment.

Carl's eyes bore through Ben as if Dr. Ji's appointment is somehow his fault.

Ignore him, Ben thinks. He says, "No problem at all, Dr. Ji. The Lightning Scalpel really speaks for itself, so I'm sure we won't need too long at all to show you how it can work for you and your team and your patients. But before we do that, I want to tell you a little bit about myself and how I got here."

Ben launches into an abbreviated version of his story of origin, in an attempt to make a connection with Dr. Ji, who, despite his brisk demeanor, has kind eyes and seems to really be taking it all in. But then Ben braves a glance at Carl during his story of origin, and Carl visibly rolls his eyes behind Dr. Ji's head.

When Ben finishes his story, he starts to focus on the presentation and get to the product itself, but Dr. Ji interrupts him. "You know, that really takes me back. When my dad broke his leg, I was only 12, but I would go with him to all his appointments because my mom was working a lot. And I was fascinated by the medical technology. It was that moment of my life when I decided to become an orthopedic surgeon. I had forgotten about that until I just heard your story." At that, Dr. Ji turns to Carl to finish this thought: "I should really share my story with my team sometime. I don't think I've ever told them that."

Carl looks briefly bewildered, but he recovers quickly to respond to Dr. Ji. "Well, yes. I think that's a great idea."

Carl glances briefly at Ben, who is careful to not make any sort of facial expression. Carl then addresses Dr. Ji again. "In fact, we just started a project at Athena where we're asking employees to share their own stories of origin. It's proven to really help employee morale and help them feel seen and heard and appreciated."

Where did he get that from? Ben wonders. *Must be Julie.*

"Is that so?" Dr. Ji asks with raised eyes. "Interesting." He turns back to Ben. "Okay, let's have it. Lightning Scalpel."

Ben nods. "Lightning Scalpel."

The rest of the pitch continues much like the Methodist Hospital pitch meeting. Not only does Ben share the impressive numbers and information, along with his favorite video, but he shares the Dr. Higgens story in a clear, concise way, and the pitch finishes under the allotted time.

Whereas Ben would've previously ended his meeting with, "That's about it. Do you have any questions?", today he tries something different. Once he is done, Ben says, "We are committed to helping you give this hospital and the people who work here the tools they need to provide the best patient care possible. If you decide to go on this journey with us, you don't just get our technology, you get our passion and skills to help your team deliver incredible patient outcomes."

There is a beat of silence as Dr. Ji nods appreciatively.

Dr. Ji then stands, and Carl and the junior executives follow suit. "Thank you, Ben and Carl. That was most informative. And entertaining. We'll be in touch." After shaking hands, Dr. Ji and his team are gone, leaving Ben and Carl alone in the conference room.

Ben quietly and quickly starts packing up his computer and notebook, but he can feel Carl watching him.

Finally, Carl speaks. "You know, Julie has told me about this storytelling thing, but I really thought it was just a gimmick. It's probably no surprise that I was not sold on the repository map or the case stories. But watching you in action there was… interesting. I don't know if it would work for everyone or every situation, but Dr. Ji certainly seemed to like it. And he's a difficult man to impress."

Ben feels like Carl isn't necessarily looking for a response here, so he just looks up and nods with a small smile, trying hard to not do anything that could be taken for an "I told you so."

They ride back down the elevator in the same silence that accompanied them up, but this time, it feels a bit more comfortable.

That Friday, Ben meets Diane at the Codependent cocktail bar downtown for a couple of hours. He recaps his Dell Senton meeting, while Diane excitedly talks about the RadarPulse and all its features. They are so deep in conversation that they don't see Zach, the Dell Senton assistant, come up behind them.

"Hey, you two!" Zack says, as Ben and Diane swivel around on their stools. They both greet Zack warmly, and Ben asks him to join them. Zack looks back at his friends and waves, and then takes a seat next to Ben.

Ben starts. "Thanks so much for coordinating the Dell Senton meeting this week. I know Dr. Ji is busy, but we made it work."

"Of course," Zack says. "It's what I do!"

Diane asks Zack what he has going on this weekend, and Zack's eyes light up with an idea. "Actually," he says, "I was going to take my buddies on a plane ride this weekend, but they just bailed. Do you both want to come? It's already planned, and the skies look perfectly clear for tomorrow."

"A plane ride?" Ben and Diane both ask in unison.

Zack laughs. "Yes. My step-dad has a Cessna at the Above and Beyond Aviation airport. He taught me how to fly years ago. I could fly that thing before I knew how to drive. I like to take it out every once in a while. It's so relaxing and fun. I'd love it if you could come."

Diane shakes her head. "Sorry, I have my sister-in-law's baby shower tomorrow."

"Too bad," Zack says, turning to Ben. "Ben?"

"I have a bike ride with my sister in the morning. What time were you thinking?"

"Does three o'clock work?"

"It does actually," Ben answers, nodding his head. "Are you sure? That's so cool."

"Absolutely sure!" Zack claps his hand on Ben's back. "I'd love the company."

"Great!" Ben says, wondering what he got himself into. "Do I need to bring anything?"

"Like what? A helmet?" Zack laughs. Actually, that's exactly what Ben is thinking.

"No, no. Just asking," Ben responds, flustered.

"Nope, I'm all good. I'll text you the directions tomorrow morning, okay?"

"Sounds good. I'm looking forward to it."

"Me, too!" Zack stands up, looking back towards his friends. "Okay, gotta go. Diane, have fun at the baby shower. Ben, see you tomorrow!"

They both say goodbye before turning back to each other. Diane raises her eyes. "A plane ride, huh?"

Ben shakes his head. "Am I crazy? It does sound fun, though."

"Sure does. I wish I could go."

"I'll tell you all about it," Ben says.

The next day, Ben pulls into the Above and Beyond Aviation parking lot, and he still can hear his sister's apprehension. Barbara was not as excited as he was when he told her about it the next morning.

Barbara yelled in her big-sister voice. "A small plane? You can't go on a small plane! You're just going to trust this guy with your life!"

And it seems that's exactly what Ben is doing.

He follows Zack's directions to park his car and finds Zack, who is on the tarmac checking the plane, right where he told Ben he'd be.

"Hi, Zack!" Ben yells through the wind as he runs up to Zack.

"Hey, Buddy!" Zack yells back with a wave.

Ben stands next to the plane while Zack completes pre-flight checks, and he is feeling very small. Not that the plane is very big, but it seems strong and powerful. It's white, with red and blue lines along each side, and Ben can't believe that soon enough it will be carrying him through the sky.

He tries to keep out of the way as Zack works his way around the plane, checking everything, before checking on everything inside the plane as well. He can't help but make a connection to his own job.

Look at the amount of preparation that goes into one flight, Ben thinks. *Am I this thorough in my preparation for each sales call? Could I do better?*

Zack is taking such care in being precise, and it's inspiring to Ben to see someone so particular and prideful.

When Zack finishes, he hops down from the plane and apologizes to Ben. "Sorry, don't want you to think I was ignoring you! My step-dad instilled in me very early on that the pre-flight checklist is the most important thing you can do for you and your plane, and I like to be thorough in my preparation."

Ben waved him off. "No apology necessary! I appreciate your thoroughness, especially since, you know, I'm going to be flying in that thing."

Zack laughs. "You'll be fine! I've been doing this forever. Plus, look at the beautiful sky!"

Ben looks up. Zack's right. It's an absolutely gorgeous day, with clear blue skies and a bit of chill in the air. He reminds himself to be present in the moment and take it all in before climbing into the co-pilot seat at Zack's command.

Once they are settled, Zack asks if Ben would like to communicate with the air traffic controller to ask for take-off. Ben momentarily panics. "What? I don't know what to say!"

"It's simple. You say three things: who you are, where you are, and where you want to go. It sounds like this: *Flight 1767 at the edge of the runway requesting clearance for takeoff. Over.*"
"That sounds very official."

"I would hope so," Zack says as he hands over the radio. Ben takes it from him and pushes the button down and says exactly what Zack told him to. He is thrilled when the air traffic controller comes over the radio and says, *Flight 1767 clear for takeoff.*"

The next thing Ben knows, Zach is taxiing down the runway, and they are airborne in seconds! What a thrill to be flying through the air, seemingly weightlessly.

It isn't easy to talk while in the air, which Ben appreciates because it gives him time to think. The request for take-off was so simple and concise, which is really all you need, and it's what people appreciate.

Ben realizes he can be more concise in his request for meetings and even for the sale. Clear, concise, compelling. It seems to make sense in all aspects of life – even flying a plane!

They cruise through the air, and occasionally Zack points at things, and Ben cranes his neck to look. He looks out the window and enjoys the feeling of flying free over buildings, trees, people. He feels so clear and relaxed and calm.

Part 8

He smells the coffee before he even gets to his cubicle on Monday morning, so he knows Diane is there, waiting. They texted Sunday about the plane ride and the baby shower, and Diane made it clear that she much would have preferred being up in the air than on the ground playing Baby Bingo.

"Hey, Diane," Ben says as he turns the corner to the cube.

Diane is, indeed, sitting in Ben's chair, staring at her phone. "Hi, Ben," she says distractedly.

"What's going on?"

"Nothing." She still hasn't looked up from her phone. "Just checking work emails. It looks like the RadarPulse tests came back, so I wanted to check them out."

"Go for it," Ben replies, as he quietly places his backpack down and maneuvers around Diane to grab his coffee.

A huge smile starts to crawl across Diane's lips.

"Well?" Ben asks, impatiently.

"It did even better than *I* expected, which is saying a lot. This is incredible! It tested so well that we're rolling it out immediately!" Diane squeals.

She finally looks up at Ben and meets his eyes. "This is going to be huge."

"Diane! That's great! I'm so happy for you. Congratulations. You deserve it."

"Thanks, Ben. I had a lot of fun working on it. I'm happy to see it all work out... and then some!"

They smile at each other and clink their coffees in a *cheers* before Diane stands and they switch places, with Ben taking a seat at his desk.

"Okay, I'm off to find Uma," Diane says. "See you later."

Ben waves and turns around to start his day.

The week goes by quietly, and before Ben knows it, it's Friday again.

He still hasn't heard a word about Dell Senton, but he knows that things tend to slow down in December. Ben has just about finished collecting case stories and stories of origins, and he is meeting with Frederico to discuss the technical logistics at two o'clock.

Right before lunch, Julie sends him a meeting invite for the same time, two o'clock that day. Ben Slacks her: *Hi, @Julie. I'm meeting with Frederico today at 2, I forgot to put it on my calendar. Do you want me to move that meeting?*

Julie writes back right away: *No need! Stop by after?*

Ben: *Will do, thanks.*

Although Julie doesn't give much away, Ben has a feeling this is about Dell Senton. He is slightly distracted in his meeting with Frederico as he visualizes yet another sale. That would be five in a row – something he's never done before.

When he knocks on Julie's open door, she calls out, "Come in! And shut the door behind you, please."

Ben does as he's told and finds Julie once again sitting in one of the two leather chairs across from her desk. He takes the one next to her and pivots a bit to face her. She doesn't have a computer or a notebook, so Ben is starting to get a little suspicious.

"Hi, Ben," Julie says, smiling.

"Good to see you, Julie. Sorry about the meeting mix-up."

"Not a problem at all. How did it go with Frederico?"

"Really great. Things are moving quickly, so we can officially launch at the start of the new year. Things are looking up!"

Julie nods, saying, "Yes, they are." She pauses and then smiles big. "And the Dell Senton sale you made is the cherry on top!"

Ben's eyes grow wide. "What? Really? It happened?!"

"It happened. Congratulations, Ben. Five sales in a row, and four of them are big ones. You really turned things around."

"Thanks, Julie. I couldn't have done without you. And Diane. I learned so much – I'm still learning so much! But I feel like I have a newfound love of my job. Even just thinking about my story of origin and where I came from. It made me appreciate this job more than ever and reminded me why I'm here."

There is silence for a few seconds, and Julie looks as if she's trying to figure out whether or not to say something.

She starts with: "And why *are* you here, Ben?"

Ben is confused. "You know the story! College, and mom, and computers—"

Julie cuts him off. "Yes, I know all that. But why are you *here*? At Athena. I know you interned here, but I'm wondering if anything else is drawing you to this particular company in general?"

Ben is totally caught off guard by this question, and he tries to quickly think of what type of response Julie could be looking for.

He starts to stumble a bit, his words falling out, "Umm, well... I... I don't... I never really..."

Julie stops him again. "No need to answer right now. Just something to think about as you continue to advance in your career."

What in the world is she talking about? Ben wonders.

"Anyway," Julie continues. "A *huge* congratulations on Dell Senton. Really. I'm so happy for you." And with that, Julie gets up and stands over Ben. Ben takes this as his cue to stand as well, and he turns towards the door as Julie moves back to her desk.

Hand on the doorknob, Ben turns back to Julie. "Thank you again, for all of the guidance and the confidence. I can't wait to see what happens next."

"Me either," Julie answers, and she sits down and starts reading emails. Ben texts Diane after work: *TGIF. Coffee tomorrow? 2 p.m. Mozart's?*

Diane writes back: *For sure. See you then.*

The next day, Ben arrives at Mozart first and heads in to grab their coffees and some doughnuts. By the time he walks back outside, Diane is already sitting at a table.

"Hey! I saw you in there, so I thought I'd grab this table."

"Perfect," Ben answers, placing the coffees and the bag down between them. He sits back in his chair and starts the business of opening the bag and laying the doughnuts out on a napkin he spreads out. As he does this, Diane asks if he heard anything about Dell Senton.

"Yes, actually," he says. "That's one of the reasons I wanted to meet you today. I talked to Julie yesterday afternoon. They said yes!"

Diane smiles wide. "Yay!" she yells. "Wonderful! Did it feel different than when you pitched them last time?"

"So different," Ben agrees. "Not only did I feel more confident, but I also felt more like myself. It felt really good. Dr. Ji loved the story of origin *and* the case story, and he even told Carl so right in the middle of the meeting."

"Wow! That must've felt good."

"Honestly, it did!"

Ben then tells Diane about the odd interaction with Julie after she told him the good news. He explains how Julie asked him why he liked working at Athena, and what drew him to the company.

"What do you think that's all about?" he asks Diane.

Diane thinks for a moment, chewing her doughnut slowly. "Hmm…

I'm not sure. Maybe she's having some sort of existential crisis thinking about her own story of origin?"

Ben nods thoughtfully. "Maybe," he says. "I don't know. It just made me feel weird. I wasn't sure what she wanted to hear, so I sort of stumbled."

"I would've done the same," Diane agrees. "I don't know how I would've answered if Uma asked me that, either."

The conversation rambled from there, and Diane and Ben talked about the different things going on in their lives: Diane's sister-in-law is about to have the baby any day now. Ben has been running with Jason more often.

Then Ben tells Diane that the girl he's been dating, Audrey, invited him to her office holiday party tomorrow night.

"Wow! That sounds serious."

"I don't know how it sounds to you, but to me, it sounds like a boring night of answering a million people asking, *So, Ben, what do you do for a living?* I hate giving the elevator pitch. I never know what to say."

Diane shakes her head and laughs. "Oh, Ben. Have I not taught you anything? You don't need an elevator pitch! You need an elevator *story*!" she exclaims.

Ben looks puzzled, and Diane continues. "So many people make the mistake of thinking that the elevator pitch is a 10-minute monologue. It shouldn't be! Remember what I said about storytelling? Stories should be clear, concise, and compelling. The goal is to intrigue people to say, *That's interesting! Tell me more.* You just need to turn your elevator pitch into a story, too. Most elevator pitches are boring and confusing. People stumble through them. You want to be inspiring, clear, and soar through your elevator story."

Ben smiles. "I should have known there would be a story in there somewhere. Now tell me, how am I supposed to do that?"

"Let's start with this. Give me your elevator pitch. Pretend we're at the party, and Audrey introduces me to you, and I ask you what you do. You say…..”

“I’m in medical equipment sales.”

“And then they fall asleep.”

“What?” Ben asks, confused.

“Nothing,” Diane rushes to move on. “What I’m saying is, that’s not exactly exciting. It doesn’t make me want to ask more. It kind of makes me want to walk away. ‘Medical equipment sales’ sounds boring and uninteresting.”

“Ouch,” Ben says, smiling. “Okay then, pitch whisperer. How would you fix it?”

“Well, first you need to start out conversational. Say something like *You know how*…. Then, describe who you help and the problem those people are having. Describe your solution, and then tell them what life is like after. Give them the resolution.”

“That sounds just like the case story structure: exposition, problem, solution, resolution.”

“That’s exactly right. Just a lot clearer and more concise. For example, if I were to give my elevator story, I would say something like: *You know how medical sales reps struggle to tell stories? I help them by bringing them coffee on Monday mornings and teaching them all about the storytelling strategies they need to close sales. After they become blackbelts in storytelling, and become friends with me, they become uber successful, and life as they know it is never the same.*”

Ben and Diane laugh, and Ben finally says, “Okay, I get it. Very funny.”

Diane smiles triumphantly and picks up her cup. “Your turn.”

“Let me think for a minute.”

They sit quietly for a bit, sipping their coffees. Diane checks her emails on her phone, while Ben stares into space. Finally, he says, “Okay, let's give it a try." Diane puts her coffee down and sits back in her chair, expectantly.

Ben begins: "You know how hospitals struggle with keeping up with the latest and greatest medical equipment? Well, I bring it right to their doorstep, selling them the most advanced equipment on the market. When they use our products, medical procedures go faster and are more successful."

Diane nods approvingly. "Really nice! That was great! So much better than," and here, she puts on a deeper voice, "*Hi, I'm Ben, I sell medical equipment.*"

Ben smiles. "Yes, I see what you mean. This is really much better. And then I'll add *I'm a life saver!*" They both laugh, remembering what Diane told her parents.

"Well, I guess now I really do have to go to Audrey's holiday party," Ben says.

"Yes, I guess so." Diane stands up and tosses her paper coffee cup in the garbage next to their table. "Okay! Got to run. My mom is waiting for me to help her set up her new cell phone." She rolls her eyes at Ben in solidarity and waves. "See you on Monday. Have fun tomorrow."

"Thanks!"

On Monday morning, Ben is checking his emails at his desk when Diane comes up behind him, Starbucks in hand. She puts his coffee on his desk, and Ben swivels in his chair. Before they even greet each other, she says, "Well, how was it last night at the holiday party?"

"It was nice! A lot of people. I did get to use the elevator story once or twice, so thank you for that. I really felt confident saying it by the end of the night."

"Good!" Diane says. "Just another tool for your toolbox."

"Absolutely. You've given me so many good tips and tricks over the past few months. I really appreciate it."

"I may have taught you a few things, but you really made them your own. You're soaring in your career now. Next year is going to bring great things. I know it."

Ben smiles. "To next year," he says, and holds out his coffee.

"To next year," Diane clinks her coffee to his.

Part 9

The holidays come and go, and before Ben knows it, it is January 2nd, and everyone is back in the office in full-swing.

Ben had a lovely Christmas with his family, and he and Diane caught up over cocktails once and coffee twice. Diane's sister-in-law had the baby, a little boy, Liam. Ben and Audrey broke up amicably. He spent New Year's Eve with Jason and Mike, and his resolution was a conglomeration of all the lessons he learned the year before: Be calm and present. Tell a story to intrigue people. Be clear, concise, and compelling. Be confident.

He walks into the office that Monday ready to put those lessons into motion again, feeling the kind of fresh that many people feel as a new year starts.

He told Diane that he would bring Monday coffees this year, so he strolls by her cubicle to find her already sitting there. She, too, is excited about a new year.

"Happy New Year!" Ben greets her.

Diane is the one to swivel now, smiling up at Ben. "Happy New Year, Ben!" She takes the hot coffee from him and has a sip. Ben notices the new addition to Diane's cubicle: A baby picture of her nephew, and he tips his coffee to it and smiles.

Diane turns to the picture. "He's a cutie."

"Sure is," Ben says. He then turns back to Diane. "Ready to have a great year?"

"Let's do it."

They wave goodbye, and Ben walks to his desk. He drops his backpack on the floor and once his computer powers up, he opens his email.

An email from Julie stands out to him. Sent yesterday, on a Sunday.

Happy New Year, Ben!

Do you want to have lunch tomorrow (Monday)? Somewhere outside of work? Maybe the Greek place around the corner? 12:30?

Julie

Ben had never had lunch with Julie. He's actually never been outside of the office with Julie before, he thinks. *What could she possibly want?* he wonders.

But of course, he can't say *no* to the boss.

I'll be there! See you at 12:30., he responds.

Ben strolls into the restaurant at 12:30 on the dot, and Julie is already seated at the table at the back. She raises her hand when he walks in, and he zig-zags around tables to get to her.

"Hi, Julie!" Ben calls out.

"Hey, Ben," Julie says more quietly. "I hope this is okay."

"Perfect! I love the food here," Ben answers as he takes a seat.

They slip into an easy conversation about their holiday break, and they are interrupted twice to order drinks and then food. Once they are done giving their food order and the waiter takes their menus, Julie turns to Ben with a serious face.

"I also did something else over the holiday break."

"Oh?" Ben asks, intrigued.

"York Surgical contacted me before the holiday break. They offered me VP of Sales, and I accepted."

Ben takes this in for a second before whisper-yelling, "Wow, Julie! That's amazing. You will be their Carl!"

Julie nods slowly, and they are both silent for a while, as Ben processes what's going on. *Julie is leaving?* He can't believe it. She seems so happy in her new role. She's such a great manager.

Julie continues. "I was definitely surprised. I had considered a move to York over the summer, but then the promotion at Athena came up, and it was so hard to say no to a raise and an office and … you get it, right?"

Ben does understand. He would do the same thing.

"And then they contacted me a few weeks ago, and I was thinking about my own story of origin and realized that I'm not exactly where I want to be yet."

Ben takes a sip of his water, letting her continue.

"No one else knows yet. I'm leaving at the end of the month. I haven't even told Carl. I have a meeting with him tomorrow." She takes a sip of her water and then puts it back down. "Please don't say anything."

"I won't," Ben says. "But why are you telling me?"

Julie looks around. Ben assumes she's making sure that no one from the office is around them. Just then, the waiter materializes with their food, and he places the hot dishes in front of them. Julie and Ben sit in silence, staring at each other over the food, not daring to move or speak until the waiter is gone.

When the waiter finally leaves, after asking if they need anything else, Julie answers. "I'm telling you because I want you to come with me."

That was *not* what Ben was expecting. He's not sure how to react, but Julie is looking at him, waiting. "Me? You want me to quit Athena?"

"Well, that's part of it, yes. But it's not about *quitting* Athena. It's about *joining* me. They said I can put my own team together. You can have what is essentially my position here, and the salary that comes with it. I know it's a leap of faith, but just look at what you and I have done. We can be amazing."

Ben takes a bite of his gyro and thinks. They *could* be amazing. Julie is right. In a short amount of time, they've led a storytelling project that has already resulted in higher sales from most of the reps in their group. Ben's sales have gone up, too, and even Carl seems to be coming around. Slightly.

But leaving Athena wasn't something that Ben had really considered. He still feels like he has more to achieve at Athena before thinking about leaving. He wants to work up the ladder, being a team player.

He realizes no one has said anything for a while. "Can I think about it?" he asks Julie. "This is a big decision."

"I *want* you to think about it! I don't want you to just jump into something, because I need to know that you are one hundred percent in and ready to make my new team be the best it can be. Take your time. Let me know by the end of the week?"

"Sure, Julie. I can do that. And thank you for asking me. You know how much I love collaborating with you, and I agree that we can do great things together. This could be a big step for both of us."

"I couldn't agree more," Julie says. And at that, it seems the conversation is over. They go back to talking about their families and their holidays, and they split the check and walk back to the office in friendly company.

Kara emails Ben on Thursday morning:

Hi, Ben! Happy New Year.

Carl would like to see you at 11:00 a.m.

Kara

Ben always finds it fascinating that it is never a question of *if* Ben could meet with Carl. It is always a given. Not like he would ever say no anyway.

At least this time, Ben isn't nervous to meet with Carl. He has Julie's offer in his back pocket, which he is now very seriously considering.

Maybe a life outside of Athena is what he needs to really reach his
potential.

As a result, walking to Carl's office isn't nearly as daunting as it used
to be. Ben greets Kara kindly, and she walks out from behind her desk
to knock on Carl's door. "Yes!" booms Carl, and Kara opens the door
and pushes Ben in, before closing it quickly behind him.

Even she seems a little scared of Carl sometimes.

Carl is, as usual, sitting behind his enormous desk, looking very
important and busy. He has a knack for always looking important and
busy, no matter what he is doing. Even when Ben sees him in line at
Starbucks some mornings, Carl looks important and busy ordering his
latte.

"Sit," Carl commands, without looking up. And then as if
remembering something, he looks up apologetically and adds,
"please."

Ben smiles and says, "Hi, Carl," as he takes a seat.

"Julie is leaving," Carl says. This is a man who doesn't do niceties.

"Oh?" Ben replies, raising his eyebrows and acting surprised.

"I know you know," Carl quickly says.

Ben drops his eyebrows immediately.

Carl explains, "When I asked her who else knew, she casually said that
she had mentioned it to you. I can only assume that means that she
wants you on her team."

"Umm…" Ben looks at his hands, feeling caught.

"No need to answer that. All I'm saying is: You have impressed me
lately."

Ben keeps looking down, afraid to meet Carl's eyes after a compliment
like that. Carl goes on: "I wasn't sold on the whole storytelling thing,
but then I saw you in action, and more, importantly, I see all the sales

you are making. Plus, you took on a leadership role in the repository map project, so I know you can work as a manager."

A manager?! Ben thinks, finally looking up at Carl just to make sure he isn't joking. But Carl isn't smiling. No surprise. Carl never smiles.

"I used the map you created. The repository map? I used it at the end-of-year sales meeting to get regional sales directors to start making introductions across divisions, as an initiative to break down silos. I can already see the results coming in, as people have been emailing me about using case stories to grow existing relationships and foster new ones. You played a huge role in that, and I can already see the benefits."

Ben is elated on the inside, hearing how Carl used the map and sees the benefits of storytelling, but he tries to keep a straight face.

Carl continues. "The bottom line is this. We need to fill Julie's role. I told you that you needed to prove yourself when you didn't get this promotion last year, and you did just that. And then some. I would like to finally offer you the regional sales manager position, along with the office and the pay that comes with it."

Flabbergasted. That's the only word Ben can think of to describe this feeling. Flabbergasted. This certainly is not what Ben was expecting to happen today.

"Are you going to say anything?" Carl finally asks.

Ben tries to find words, but words are hard. "Thank you. That's very kind of you."

Carl nods, waiting for Ben to say more.

Ben's mind is racing. He knows that Carl is looking for an immediate response, because that's how Carl is. But Julie's offer is hanging in the air, too.

I need to say something, Ben thinks, as the silence looms over both of them.

"Can I… think about it?" he manages.

"Of course you can," Carl responds. "I'm a reasonable man." Ben searches Carl's face for a hint of sarcasm, but he can't find any. "Tomorrow."

Ben blinks slowly and then nods his head. "Tomorrow. I'll email Kara."

"No need," Carl says. "I'll be waiting. 10 a.m."

"Thank you. Really, thank you very much for considering me and for recognizing my hard work."

"You're welcome, Ben. See you tomorrow." Carl turns to his computer, and it seems that's the end of the conversation. Ben lets himself out and gives Kara a small wave before walking back to his cubicle. He feels like he's walking through a fog, his mind racing a mile a minute.

When he gets back to his desk, he texts Diane immediately to let her know what just happened. He already told her about his meeting with Julie (even though Julie swore him to secrecy), so he knows that Diane would appreciate the new turn of events: *Just met with Carl. He offered me Julie's position.*

Diane texts back: *Seriously?! Yay! I think I've created a monster!*

Ben laughs to himself and puts his phone away. He doesn't know how he's going to make this decision, especially by tomorrow morning. Ben marvels at how he was worried about being fired not too long ago, and now he has his dream promotion at not one but two places.

He needs to talk to someone who can be objective and help him weigh his options.

Later that day, Ben tells Barbara what happened over the phone. She tells him to come over for dinner so she can help him talk it through. Barbara is the quintessential big sister, and she is always the one that Ben turns to when he needs advice.

Barbara opens the door before Ben can even knock. "Hey, brother!" she says. "I'm so happy for you. Two offers in one week!"

"Thanks, Barbara," Ben says, walking through the door and taking off his coat. Where's Clara?"

"Washing up for dinner. I made mom's lasagna."

Ben cuts and serves the lasagna while Barbara probes him with more questions than he's ever answered in his life: questions about his work and personal goals, his management style, his relationship with Julie, his "relationship" with Carl (if you could even call it that). Ben does his best to answer her questions honestly and thoughtfully because he knows that, as annoying as it may seem, Barbara always has a method to her madness, and she really is one of the most level-headed people he knows. She'll help him figure out the right answer.

As dinner comes to an end, they have some decaf coffee and Clara's lunchbox cookies. Dave has left the table to put Clara to bed, but Barbara and Ben are still sitting at the table, talking through this decision.

Ben shakes his head and says for the hundredth time, "I just can't believe this is happening. This is exactly what I wanted. And if it wasn't for Diane, I would never be here. She taught me all about storytelling, and it's the reason my career took off."

Barbara smiles. "It's a shame she's not getting promoted, too."

And just like that, the answer is perfectly clear to Ben.

At ten on the dot the next morning, Ben stands in front of Kara's desk. "Carl is expecting me."

Kara waves him in without a word, and Ben clears his throat to make his presence known before entering the office and shutting the door behind him.

Carl looks up at Ben and nods to the chair across from him. Ben takes a seat, and Carl still hasn't said a word. Apparently, Ben has to be the first one to talk.

"Thank you again for offering me that promotion, Carl," he begins.

Silence.

Ben goes on. "I thought about it all night, and I would like to negotiate something."

Carl's eyebrows raise. He looks both surprised and impressed, and Ben doubts that many people attempt to negotiate with Carl.

Ben says, "I know that I have become a stronger salesperson, and I know that I will continue to improve and win sales. I also know that I will be a great manager and will teach my team how to become irresistible through storytelling."

Silence.

"I also know that I wouldn't be here today without the help of Diane, my senior solutions engineer. She is the one who taught me about storytelling. She knows everything there is to know about the equipment, but she always knows how to build up the soft skills that anyone needs to make a sale."

Silence.

"I love it here at Athena. As you know, I interned here in college, and this was my first and only job after. But before I make my final decision, I would like to propose that Diane also gets a promotion, so we can move up together and continue creating a better and more successful workforce."

Carl is so still he could be a statue, but his eyes have a far-away look that could only mean that he's processing what Ben has just proposed.

Ben knows that it was risky to negotiate with Carl, but he also knows that he could not accept a promotion at Athena without Diane also being recognized for her hard work. He wouldn't be where he was, sitting across from Carl, with a promotion within his reach, without Diane. He also wouldn't have been offered a position from Julie without Diane.

But Ben isn't ready to leave yet. After talking to Barbara, he decided to think of himself as a stock and invest in doubling down on the relationships he has built with his clients and co-workers at his current job. He still has work to at Athena, and with Diane at his side, he is giddy about the possibilities.

When Carl finally speaks, he simply says, "Let me talk to Uma. I'll be in touch."

Ben thanks him and quickly takes his leave before Carl can say anything else.

At four o'clock, Kara Slacks Ben: *Can you come by the office?* Of course, Ben knows exactly what office Kara means. Carl's made his decision.

When Ben gets there, though, Carl's door is closed. Kara tells him to go in anyway, so Ben knocks and then opens the door slowly. He sees Carl sitting at his desk, assuming his usual position, but there are two more people there, too: Uma is standing next to Carl, behind the desk, and Diane is sitting in one of the two chairs across from Carl.

No one's face seems to give anything away, and Carl asks Ben to close the door and take a seat.

Uma starts. "Diane, Carl spoke to me about the wonderful job you have been doing here at Athena. It is clear that you have been reaching across the aisle and helping everyone become the best they can be, through your lessons on storytelling."

Uma pauses, and Diane doesn't move. Ben's not sure where this is going yet.

Carl then says, "Diane, I offered Ben a promotion. Julie's job, after she leaves us at the end of the month. He said that he would accept only if you, too, were promoted, so the two of you could work on company-wide initiatives to improve sales through storytelling."

Diane looks at Ben, surprised. Ben didn't want to tell her before now, just in case it didn't work out, so she really did not see this coming.

Uma continues. "And it turns out, I was already drafting a proposal for your promotion when Carl talked with me this morning. You've been so successful here at Athena that we would love to have both of you in management positions."

Uma hands Diane a paper, and Ben assumes it's the details of the promotion. Diane's eyes scan the paper quickly, and she smiles.

Looking up at Uma, Diane says, "Thank you very much. I love working here at Athena." Then she looks at Ben, still smiling, but continues speaking to Uma. "And I would be happy to accept."

"Yes!" Ben yells softly before he can help himself. It's his turn to speak. "Carl. Uma. Thank you both. Diane and I have a lot of work to do, and it's going to be great having a friend to do that with. I know whoever tells the best story is the one that will get the sale. We have great stories to share with the team, where our clients are the heroes, and I know we can continue to create new ones together, too."

Carl and Uma both look at each other and then back at Ben and Diane. Uma smiles and nods, and Carl simply says, "We look forward to it."

Resolution

Ben walks through Diane's open office door on Monday morning, coffees in hand. It's April, and it's also the day of their first company-wide sales training.

Since they began their new jobs in February, Ben and Diane have been working together on a storytelling sales initiative to present to all sales reps in Q2, and today is the day. They even ordered t-shirts that say "The Sale Is in the Tale," which they will be handing out at the door.

After this meeting, Ben and Diane will be writing a sales training program based on their takeaways and those of the participants.

When they first went to Carl and Uma with this idea, they were immediately on board, and all four of them are excited to see morale and sales improve through the end of the year.

Ben sinks down into the chair across from Diane's desk. He smiles at the pictures of her nephew on the desk and reaches over to hand her the coffee: black, hot, as always.

Diane takes the coffee. "Thanks, Ben," she says, and holds it out to cheers.

"Cheers," they both clink paper coffee cups.

"To us!" Diane says.

And Ben replies, "And to the stories yet to be told!"

By the end of the full-day meeting, Ben once again takes the podium and looks out at all of the sales reps sitting before him. More than half of them put their t-shirt on over their work clothes, and they look happy and excited, as they expressed during the break-out groups that they were looking forward to using the stories they heard today and creating their own stories.

It's now up to Ben to close the meeting, and he ends with: "Now you know how to grow your business beyond your previous success. We've learned about how to create interesting elevator stories. We discussed our stories of origin. We talked about Athena's company values and how to incorporate those into our sales. And most importantly, we learned about case stories and honed our storytelling skills to make sure the story is clear, concise, and compelling. And memorable! And as a result, we have created that playlist of stories that we can pull from at any time to fit the type of buyer we are working with."

Here, Ben pauses and takes a breath, being present in the moment and marveling at how far he and Diane have come.

"To be the best and stay on top, you must let go of the old way of selling and pushing out information. The new way of selling is to tell stories that pull people in and make you irresistible. Together, we will start using storytelling to become revenue rockstars."

Everyone claps, and Ben ends with an important take-away: "Remember: The Sale Is in the Tale!"

Five Storytelling Secrets: Methodology

Use these templates to practice the five storytelling secrets that Ben learns to stop from drowning in the sea of sameness. Increase your storytelling skills, just as Ben does, because when you increase your storytelling skills, your sales go up proportionally. The better the story you learn to tell, the higher the odds of making the sale.

Secret 1: The Elevator Story

Let's kill the elevator pitch right here and now. They are usually so boring and robotic. Ben is tired of giving the same old boring elevator pitch at events and meetings, and Diane helps him craft his elevator story to keep people interested and asking for more.

Most people make the mistake of thinking that the elevator pitch is a 10-minute monologue. It is not! It should be clear, concise, and compelling. In fact, this should be your checklist for any story you tell!

- Is it clear? This is crucial because *the confused mind always says no* without telling you they are confused.
- Is it concise? People should be able to remember it and share it.
- Is it compelling? Your elevator story should have an emotional hook, so people feel connected to you.

The goal is to intrigue people so that they say, "That's interesting! Tell me more."

Most elevator pitches are boring and confusing. People stumble through them. You want to be inspiring and clear, and be able soar through your elevator STORY using these five steps.

1. Start a conversation with "You know how…?"

2. Describe who you help.

3. Describe the problem people are having (Hint: Use the word *struggle* in the description).

4. Describe your solution.

5. End with the resolution: What is life like for these people after they've worked with you?

When you have a great elevator pitch, people may want to hire you on the spot, or they will remember what you do and send you referrals! Do you see how the first three steps will really make you stand out? Most people say *I'm in medical sales* or *I am a lawyer* or *I am a financial advisor*. Using the storytelling method, you don't get to your solution until step 4!

Here is my elevator story:

You know how many salespeople in healthcare and technology struggle to stand out in a sea of sameness when they pitch against competitors? They push out facts and figures and wonder why they keep coming in second place.

After winning Salesperson of the Year at Conde Nast and writing four books on the power of storytelling, I've become known as 'The Pitch Whisperer.' After people hear my keynote, they learn to tell stories that tug at heartstrings which causes people to open their purse strings. They start winning new business because they tell the best story.

Secret 2: Story of Origin

When Ben considers how he got to where he is, he realizes how much passion he has always had for the job—passion that he didn't know existed before he was asked for his story of origin.

His story of origin allows him to connect with both colleagues and clients about their shared dedication and excitement.

When considering your own story of origin, use these questions to get the ball rolling.

1. Why am I in this industry?

2. Think back to childhood or when you were deciding what you wanted to major in in school. Was there any indication that you would wind up here?

3. Why do you like to do what you do?

4. Who is it that you help?

And remember to ask your potential buyers their own story of origin. Rarely is anyone's path linear and even rarer still, you will be asking them for a story that few others even think to ask. When potential buyers or clients share their story of origin with you, it is a bonding moment in which you listen, so they feel seen, heard, and even appreciated for what they had to overcome to get to where they are now.

Here is my story of origin:

Growing up in the suburbs of Chicago, I was always fascinated by what motivates people to take action, so I majored in advertising. After a 15-year sales career at Conde Nast, where I won Salesperson of the Year, I learned that whoever told the best story got the sale. Now my passion is helping as many people as possible get off the self-esteem roller coaster of only feeling good if they are meeting their goals and bad about themselves if they miss a goal. As a sales keynote speaker, I love helping people become storytellers as a new way to connect and get new clients.

Secret 3: The Company Story

Ben learns that by telling not just his own story, but also the company's story, he is able to make valuable emotional connections. Consider your own company's story. (Even if that company is you!)

Focus on values, the culture, and your favorite part of work. Don't focus on how many years you've been there or how long you've studied.

Use this template to create your story:

1. What got you into this industry? (Hint: Use the story of origin template!)

2. What do you love about your job?

3. Who in your industry inspires you?

4. What are the core values of your company (or you)?

5. How do you embody those values? The ability to have a story of the values in action will make it so much more than just something on the website.

6. How do you give back to your community?

Even if you just work for yourself, you have a company and a brand.

The Pitch Whisperer is my brand and the values are passion, integrity, and joy. That is the compass I use on which to base my actions and the types of people I want to work with as a speaker and sales trainer.

Secret 4: Case Stories

Diane helps Ben create intriguing case stories that pull people in and allow them to see themselves in the story.

Case studies are typically boring and dry, with facts and figures. Turning a case study into a case story is going to be your secret sauce to winning new business.

Case stories tug at people's heartstrings, which causes them to open their purse strings. They also make you memorable, intriguing, and shareable.

(Note: Take a look at your existing testimonials. Are they telling a story, or are they just saying something generic? Remember: People have to see themselves in the case story in order to say *yes*.)

Here are four steps you can take to create a case story.

1. Exposition: These are the "who, what, when, where" details. Think of yourself as a journalist. You need to paint the picture to get people into the story.

2. Problem: The better you describe the problem, the more people think you have their solution. The stakes have to be high to get people to care.

3. Solution: You should describe what makes you unique. Explain where you got the skills to provide a solution that is proven to work.

4. Resolution: This is the secret sauce to any great story. What is life like for the people you help after you've provided your product or service? What is it that makes them so happy they hired or bought from you? Usually, this is the outcome of the transformation from feeling *overwhelmed* or *stressed* to now

being *calm* and *happy*. That's when the pain point is solved.

Remember: *The Wizard of Oz* did not end with the *solution* of Dorothy getting in the balloon to go home. Instead, it has a wonderful *resolution* scene where she realizes how wonderful the people in her life are. Tell a story that has your *Wizard of Oz moment* and you'll be telling stories that become a classic, too!

Here is one of my favorite case stories:

In 2020, Olympus Medical reached out to me because they wanted to have storytelling become part of their marketing and sales culture. They realized their sales team and marketing materials were lacking any emotional context and were struggling to gain market share.

Having me as their keynote speaker was the kick-off to this new shift. Once we did a deep dive on turning their features into compelling stories, they started to see the doctors becoming more willing to say yes faster to what they were offering.

After my talk and workshop, their entire team of over 200 salespeople went through my online course, which further developed their storytelling skills. Now they share case stories with each other and across other divisions, so they are getting revenue from both winning new business and growing existing clients.

Secret 5: Playlist of Stories

Once you have your story of origin, company story, and case stories, it's time to build! Create a repository of stories, or a playlist from which you can draw from at any time. Trade stories with your colleagues or mentors.

Consider 3-5 different avatars of clients, and create a repository of case stories to draw from for each type. For instance, some people respond better to:

Emotions
Numbers
Facts/figures
Pictures
Nostalgia

The more stories you have to pull from, the more likely you are to have a story that fits the person sitting across from you. For example, depending on whether I am talking to an event planner or a CEO, I have different case stories ready to go that fit their criteria on what speaker they will hire.

This is an ongoing process that continues to evolve. The key is to start with what you have, and then look at what is missing so you know exactly what case story you need to develop.

This keeps you fully present and on your toes. Instead of just giving the same pitch to everyone, you will be searching your "playlist" of stories to see which is the right one that will resonate most with your potential buyer.

The more you embrace storytelling, the more energized you will become. Remember: people buy your energy so tell your stories with as much passion as possible. It is the first time for the potential buyer to hear it!

Acknowledgments

This book is dedicated to my sister Barbara and our Mom, Trish: the people who always have my back and cheer me on!

Special thanks to Cristen Fitzpatrick, who is my co-pilot in storytelling, which includes everything from helping craft and edit this book to running my online course "Revenue Rockstar Mastery" and managing my social media. Her contributions to this book made the whole process fun and take flight.

Also huge thanks to Shawn Ellis for his guidance on my speaking career and branding and for inspiring me to write this fable. Special thanks to the incredible team at Executive Speakers Bureau including Stephen Kirkpatrick, Jennifer Lier, Jenny Foreman, and Richard, Angela, and Carson Schelp.

To my publisher and publicist, Steve Rohr, who has been an incredible supporter for over 17 years. What can I say but thanks! Shout-out to my talented friend Sergio Belletini who designed the front cover. Many thanks to my fellow keynote speaker and Austinite, Erik Qualman, for his insightful foreword.

Thanks to the many marketing and sales executives who, over the years, have trusted and hired me to be the keynote speaker at their sales meetings. Your willingness to share your challenges and new victories you have won from learning how to tell better stories are what gives this book texture and authenticity.

Finally, a group of friends who are characters in my story that enrich my life: Ken Baker; Alyce Alston; Sameer Somal; Josh Linkner; Nina Lawrence; Phillip Sherman; Amber Allen; George and Travis Baxter-Holder; Tim Francis; Amanda Russell; Sean and Rebecca Scanlon; Cynthia Lieberman; Katherine Willis; Judith Light; James Mellon; Kevin Bailey; Natasha King; Dr. Michael Breus; Richard Ayoub; Brad Bessey; Ken Rutkowski; Sandy Grigsby; Will Henshall; Sanyika Street; Glenn and Kristen Hemanes; Claudio and Rachel Ludovisi; Jason and Mary Azevedo; Jim, Karen, and Andrew Kallimani; Gabrielle Berberich; Ishmael Jackson; Sheila Burns; Paul, David, Laura, Jim, and Debby Livesay; Ken Sky; Dan Burrus; Marcus Bell; Rob Angel; Tony Grebmeier; Dr. Mark Goulston; Dr. Benjamin Ritter; Ben Woodward; Sterling Hawkins; John Ruhlin; Isaac Lidsky; Dr. Keri Stephens; Beth Cuzzone; David Freeman, J.D.; Tom and Tracy Hazzard; Emmanuel Mercapidez; and Elaine Gordon.

About the Author

John Livesay, aka The Pitch Whisperer, is a sales keynote speaker where he shows companies' sales teams how to turn mundane case studies into compelling case stories so they win more new business. From John's award-winning career at Conde Nast, he shares the lessons he learned that turns sales teams into revenue rock stars. His TEDx talk, *Be the Lifeguard of Your Own Life*, has over 1,000,000 views.

Clients love working with John because of his ongoing support after his talks, which can include implementing the storytelling skills from his online course Revenue Rockstar Mastery. The need for storytelling continues to grow and has led to a number of companies in healthcare, technology, insurance, mortgage, food and beverage, real estate, travel, and automotive to bring John in to speak to their sales teams.

John is a guest lecturer on how to leverage the power of storytelling in sales at multiple universities including the University of Texas at Austin, Pepperdine Graziadio Business school, and University of Chicago Booth School of Business.

He is also the host of "The Successful Pitch" podcast, which is heard in over 60 countries. These interviews make him a sales keynote speaker with fresh and relevant content. Fortune and INC have done articles on John's concept of being "stuck in the friend zone" at work. He has appeared on TV including the KTLA morning show and Yahoo Finance on the power of storytelling.

John currently lives in Austin with Pepe, his King Charles Spaniel, who reminds him every day of the importance of belly rubs.

To learn more about having John as a speaker at your next event, please visit johnlivesay.com.